The Thirsty Dragon

Lyn Ebenezer

Gwasg Carreg Gwalch

Cover design: Sian Parri
ISBN: 1-84527-048-7

Gwasg Carreg Gwalch,
12 Iard yr Orsaf, Llanrwst, Conwy, Cymru (Wales)
LL26 0EH
Tel: 01492 642031 Fax: 01492 641502
e-mail: books@carreg-gwalch.co.uk website: www.carreg-gwalch.co.uk
Printed and published in Wales.

Acknowledgements (illustrations, by page number):

National History Museum, Wales: 7, 23, 57, 59, 69, 91, 95, 110

The author's collection: 27, 29

Gwasg Carreg Gwalch: 13, 14, 15, 17, 19, 20, 25, 30, 33-48, 49, 61, 66, 68, 71, 72, 87,
88, 99, 100, 105, 107, 109, 113, 114

Fferm Fêl y Ceinewydd: 11

Baner ac Amserau Cymru: 51, 52

Brains: 65

W. Alister Williams: 80, 85

Archifdy Gwynedd: 99

THE THIRSTY DRAGON

Contents

There are many good reasons for drinking,
And one has just entered my head;
If a fellow can't drink when he's living,
How the hell can he drink when he's dead?

Anon

Introduction

Very little has been published on the history of the brewing industry and the social phenomenon of beer drinking in Wales. Apart from the occasional book by experts like Brian Glover, the subject has been largely ignored. Glover's classic *The Prince of Ales* has been invaluable to my research.

Today, only two major breweries remain in Wales, a very different situation to that which existed only a century ago, when every town or city worth the name housed its own brewery. Beer – whether regarded as the elixir of life or the demon drink – was central to Welsh life, and brewing was an important industry. It was part of everyday life. There was a time when beer claimed its place on the table at meal times as naturally as did bread, butter and cheese.

This volume traces the history of alcohol-making and brewing from pre-Ancient Egyptian days through the era of the Druids to the present day. It is likely that the first alcoholic drink was mead, and the honey-based beverage played an important part in Welsh society at the time of the Gododdin, featured in a poem by Aneirin describing a battle fought in 600 AD. Mead also featured prominently in the Courts of the Welsh Princes.

I attempt in this book to trace the tradition of brewing, starting with the 'macsu' or home brewing, which was once prevalent throughout Wales but is now confined to areas of Pembrokeshire. At one time, every farm or homestead would brew its own beer, while the large country mansions built their own private breweries. Then came the first industrial breweries, which were opened to meet the ever-increasing need to quench the thirst of steel workers and miners. This, in turn, sparked the temperance movement. Today it is difficult to imagine that the abbeys were Wales' premier breweries.

The volume also touches on several lesser-known aspects of alcohol production and consumption in Wales, ranging from the intention by Arthur Guinness of moving his Dublin brewery to north Wales, and the claim that a Welshman invented Ireland's national drink, to the only Drinkers' Union that was ever established – Undeb y Tancwyr. Did you know that the brewery featured in S4C's soap opera, *Pobol y Cwm* is filmed in a working brewery in Cardiff? Where is the world's smallest brewery? Which brewery celebrates the memory of Buddy Holly? They are both in Wales. Did you know that Felinfoel Brewery near Llanelli was the first in Europe to supply beer in cans? Who could believe that Buckley's Reverend James beer was named after a minister of religion who set up the brewery, and that Wrexham was at one time the most important brewing town in Britain?

It is only natural that I have chosen to extend the account to include spirits, from the first-ever Welsh whisky distillery near Bala, to today's Penderyn whisky. Welsh cider is also featured.

Alcohol has been both championed and cursed by our bards. While T. Gwynn Jones sang of the merits of golden mead, during the Great War Lloyd George regarded alcohol as more of an enemy to Wales than all of

The old brewery at Builth Wells, long since closed

Some of the brewers and distilleries of Wales

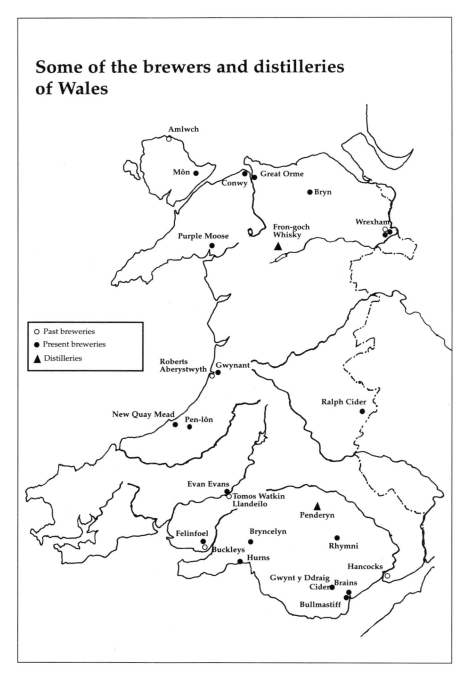

Amlwch

Môn ●

Great Orme

Conwy

● Bryn

Wrexham

Purple Moose
●

Fron-goch
Whisky
▲

○ Past breweries
● Present breweries
▲ Distilleries

Roberts
Aberystwyth
○ ● Gwynant

New Quay Mead
●

Pen-lôn
●

Ralph Cider

Evan Evans
○ Tomos Watkin
Llandeilo

▲
Penderyn

Felinfoel
○ Buckleys

Bryncelyn
●

Rhymni
●

Hurns
●

Hancocks
○

Gwynt y Ddraig Brains
Cider ● ●

Bullmastiff

Old Welsh cider drinking vessels

Germany's U-boats put together.

I have attempted to provide an up-to-date account of working alcohol makers in Wales by using CAMRA's list of Welsh brewers and the Welsh Perry and Cider's list of Welsh cider makers. However, it is quite possible that some of the listed producers are no longer in business and that I have unwittingly omitted others. For this, I apologise.

This version of the history of brewing, distilling and meading in Wales is dedicated to Undeb y Tancwyr, the only trade union not ever to contemplate going on strike. So, fill your glasses and raise them to the beloved tipple.

Iechyd da!

Lyn Ebenezer
Summer 2006

Chapter 1

The Nectar of the Gods

Mead is regarded as being the first alcoholic tipple ever to be tasted by man or woman and it has a history that stretches back at least five thousand years. It is a drink made from honey, a basic source of food that has benefited humans from the very beginning.

Mead is simply unique in that its consumption spurned social divisions. It was drunk by the common people, by their rulers and by their gods. In Germanic legend, mead was a one-way ticket to Asgard, the Land of the Gods, and Asgard was the imbiber's heaven. Not only would drinking mead ensure your passage there, but in Asgard more mead would be awaiting the new arrivals, who would share it with Odin, Honir, Lokir and Thiasi and all their other godly mates.

Well before the beginning of Christianity, the Teutons believed that mead could awaken the senses and cure all ills, but there was one drawback for mere mortals: they could not concoct the perfect tipple until they reached the promised land. Once there, however, mortals would become perfect mead-makers.

In its simplest form, mead is merely a honey wine made from a mixture of honey and water and left to ferment. It is quite possible that it was first created accidentally when drops of rain fell into a pot of honey and particles of wild yeast were blown into the mixture by the wind. Perhaps someone somewhere then decided to drink the mixture rather than throw it away, and that unknown person became the world's first alcoholic imbiber. The rest, as they say, is history.

Mead has had celebratory connections from the very beginning. It is closely associated with various ancient marriage ceremonies – including pre-nuptial ceremonies, the marriage itself, and post-nuptial traditions. It has a direct connection with the word 'honeymoon', known in Welsh as 'mis mêl', which literally means 'honey month'. In Norwegian, the word for honeymoon is 'hjunottsmanathr'. Try saying that after a few cups of mead. It relates to the custom in Western Europe, including Wales, of kidnapping the future bride and hiding her for some specific period of time. In Scandinavian legend, the 'honeymoon' consisted of the custom in which the newly-weds, during their first month – or moon – together, would drink a cup of mead each and every day. There is evidence of such customs existing at the time of Attila the Hun, who lived between approximately 406 and 453 AD. Not usually known for his sweeter nature, should he, perhaps, be renamed Attila the Honey?

The references to mead in the Laws of Hywel Dda indicate its importance in Wales in the tenth century and since

In ancient Israel, there was a custom in which the bride and groom spent some time hidden away together in a secluded spot where they would drink a concoction known as bride's beer, which was made from fermented honey.

Mead is strongly associated with the Celts. In Celtic culture it reigned above any other form of drink. One ancient Welsh law insisted that a mead cask should measure the breadth of nine hands and be wide enough to bathe both the king and one of his advisors. Mead is thought to have been made in Wales since at least 600 AD. The arrival of the Romans failed to interrupt the making and drinking of mead. Indeed, the Romans brought their own wine with them and began adding honey to sweeten their recipe.

Mead was the drink of Welsh castles and courts. Poets and minstrels sang paeans of praise to it. One such poem praises Sycharth, the court of Owain Glyndŵr, for its bread and cheese, beer and meat.

There is a strong possibility that mead lay behind the quarrels between the Britons and the Saxons. Because the Britons could brew better and stronger mead, the Saxons took revenge by stealing their lands and belongings.

Mead played an important part in the Battle of Catterick, which was fought around 595-600 AD in north Yorkshire. Before battle, the king,

Mynyddog Mwynfawr, prepared enough mead for his army of three hundred Welsh soldiers to drink for a whole year before they marched from Din-Eitin, where Edinburgh stands today. Against huge odds, they slaughtered seven times their own number and only three of Mynyddog's men survived, but it was regarded as a victory for the Britons. In early Welsh literature, a good soldier would be described as one who was 'worth his mead'.

The many references to mead by the Bards of the Princes reflects the social importance of the drink. Because of its strong carbohydrate content, mead was taken by soldiers before battle to add to their strength and accelerate their recovery. Mynyddog Mwynfawr must have known this. Such was the importance of mead that the mead-maker or brewer was placed eleventh in the hierarchy of the king's officers. He enjoyed the same status as the court doctor.

Ynys Môn (Anglesey) was renowned for its mead and its mead-makers. The island was home to numerous courts, among them Rhosyr, Aberffraw and Penrhosllugwy. All these courts had their bards, and lands were given to them throughout the island, such as those at at Gwalchmai, Trefeilyr and Llanfihangel Tre'r Beirdd. The place-name Llannerch-y-medd has a special significance. It means the Glade of the Mead. Indeed, the very word 'medd' – which is Welsh for mead – is the root of the Welsh word for being drunk – 'meddw'.

By the beginning of the twentieth century, mead had lost its social status, and getting drunk on mead was regarded as something that was most detrimental to the body. In July 1932 Evan Roberts of Llandderfel wrote in *Yr Haul* (The Sun), the journal of the Church in Wales:

> ... to be drunk from drinking mead was a drunkenness appallingly harmful to the body, and it was a drunkenness of the kind that one would not sober from for many days. Besides, its effect on the balance of the body was very different to drunkenness caused by ale. When one gets drunk on ale, he leans forwards, until the drunkard goes head first, but the mead would [make one] lean backwards, and that drunkard was forced to go 'back to front' despite all efforts to go forward.

Evan Roberts, incidentally, demonised mead in order to minimise the criticism of drinking the ale and beer that was brewed by the church.

The temperance movement, of course, had as its aim a ban on all alcoholic drinks. Yet mead was not demonised by the religious revivalists to the same extent as ale and beer. In *Life and Tradition in Rural Wales*, J.

Honeycombs exhibited at the New Quay Honey Farm

Geraint Jenkins maintains that mead drinking did not come to be seen as one of the deadly sins. He describes the process of mead-making, which took place in late summer:

> The ingredients of mead were honeycombs with the honey removed, cold water, hops and yeast. Cold water was poured on the honeycombs. And the mixture was allowed to steep overnight. On the following day it was strained through a fine sieve into a boiler to be boiled very slowly. The surface of the liquid was skimmed frequently, a handful of hops was added and after boiling for another quarter of an hour the liquid was allowed to cool to blood temperature. A pint of brewer's yeast was then added and left for some hours. Usually the mead was bottled in stone jars that had to be buried in a marshy field for at least six months before it was considered fit to drink.

Even though over the centuries mead lost its popularity to other alcoholic drinks, it survived. Today there are increasing signs that it is well on its way back to popularity. At the Royal Welsh Show, there is an annual increase in the number and standard of mead exhibits. It seems to be making a comeback in all the Celtic countries, especially in Cornwall. In Wales, its popularity was boosted when the New Quay Honey Farm was opened in 1995 at Cross Inn on the Ceredigion coast. Here, the links with the past have been renewed by the making of mead, which is fermented naturally in a purpose-built mead-house. The fermentation takes place at ordinary summer temperature in order to retain the taste of fresh honey throughout the process. The liquid is then kept in oak casks for between three and six months. The aim is to make a mead whose production is simple, but which is complex in its subtle taste, retaining the flavour and goodness of pure honey.

There is a wide choice of meads and honey products available now. Sweet and medium honey meads are sold at the farm shop, as are meads flavoured with various fruits. The result is a modern mead with a unique taste, a resuscitation of the traditional alcoholic drink that was lauded in medieval Welsh verse, and that was the drink of Welsh Princes and the peasantry alike.

Honey beer is also brewed in the traditional manner at New Quay Honey Farm, with honey used to accentuate the taste and strength of the beer. Little honey is actually added, but it adds significantly to the light flavour. Despite the addition of honey, the beer is not too sweet.

New Quay's Honey Farm has developed into a centre that specialises in honey in all its aspects, a place where visitors are encouraged to observe the various processes carried out both by humans and bees.

Heather mead produced at the New Quay Honey Farm

Guto'r Glyn and Gutyn Owain and many other bards of the Middle Ages praised the hospitality extended at Valle Crucis Abbey

Chapter 2

Holy Ale and Home Brew

In the Welsh language, no distinction is made between ale and beer. In English, however, ale was always regarded as a fermented drink containing malt but brewed without hops, while beer would contain hops. Today, that distinction has largely disappeared, and ale has become nothing more than a trade word.

The term 'home brew' can also be misleading. It is naturally assumed by many to be ale or beer that is brewed in the home. However, home brew was not only brewed in people's houses, but was also an important part of monastic life. An early 'brewer', Saint Kevin of Glendalough in County Wicklow in Ireland (498-618), is reputed to have miraculously turned water into ale. Nevertheless, neither history nor legend suggests that it was ale that was responsible for his longevity – he lived to 120. Others were less gifted, and had to use more practical methods.

As far back as 800 AD, religious institutions encouraged the consumption of a certain amount of beer and wine. Saint Benedict of Aniane, for example, stipulated that the amount of beer allowed in his religious houses was double that of wine. During fast-days, bread and some salt was allowed with water or beer. In 813 AD the Aix Chapelle Council permitted the canons four litres of ale daily while some nunneries allowed their nuns as much as seven litres a day.

On the continent, and in France especially, brewing and making wine and spirits were monastic industries, as natural a part of monastic life as cheese-making, while in the south of France, cider-making was a daily occurrence. The abbey brewery was just as important as the abbey kitchen or bakery. It was a natural progression for in-house brewing and distilling to develop into a business whose product was sold to the world beyond. In one abbey in Switzerland, three breweries stood within the abbey's jurisdiction, but only one of these supplied the abbey itself. Typical abbey breweries would have a malt house and a cold store for fermentation. Indeed, unofficially, abbeys would compete with each other for the right to boast the best brew. The later development of beer-making from ordinary ale-making is attributed to these monks.

It can also be said that monks invented the double-bottomed vat. This device enabled two successive infusions of the mash to be used; the second infusion produced 'small beer', which was drunk by novices, poor pilgrims and nuns. 'Small beer' has remained as a dismissive term for something insignificant.

During the eleventh and twelfth centuries, abbeys in Wales also brewed proficiently and profusely. At Llanddewi Nant Hodni (Llanthony) the monks would brew not only for their own consumption but also for visiting travellers. It was there that the custom of marking casks with crosses to note the strength of the drink originated. There were also clear guidelines as to the etiquette of drinking. Those monks who tended to dribble while singing were sent to their beds without supper.

Indeed, during this period, there was hardly a monastic institution without its brewing facilities. At the Priory in Carmarthen a brewery stood between the kitchen and the buttery. Visiting travellers had to make do with weak beer, while the best tipple was reserved for the Abbot and the monks of the higher orders.

In *The Welsh Cistercians*, David H. Williams notes that brewing was common at Strata Florida, Maes Glas (Basingwerk) and Margam Abbeys:

> Every sizeable medieval abbey had its brew-house producing various grades of ale, useful for the communities at their daily 'drinkings', but also for sale. The troubles with the Welsh *conversi* in the late 12th century stemmed in part from excessive consumption of beer. Margam produced its 'strong beer' and Tintern its 'better beer', but it also had 'dregs' left over, once stolen from its brewery…. There was poetic praise for the 'home brewed cider, mead and bragget' of Strata Marcella (c. 1490). Basingwerk sold beer in Holywell ….

Y Gegin Fawr, Aberdaron – a stop for pilgrims bound for Enlli

In their last decades, if not much earlier, a 'tavern house' stood at Llantarnam Abbey's Penrhys shrine; an ale-house stood within the precincts of Strata Florida, and grain for malt was ground in the mills of Vale Royal and Whitland.

At Tintern, the abbey granted licenses to tenants who wished to sell commodities for a fee of six pence, but this charge was doubled if beer was sold. At this abbey, one tenant's surname is listed as 'Beremaker'.

There is an interesting anecdote about an event at Strata Florida Abbey in 1195. Following a drunken skirmish between some of the abbey's *conversi*, or lay brothers and their counterparts at Abbey Cwm Hir, a problem referred to above by David H. Williams, the Strata Florida monks were exiled for a time to Clairvaux in western France. Clairvaux was the daughter church of Citeax and was the mother church to Whitland Abbey, while Whitland, in turn, was Strata Florida's mother church. According to historical records, the Strata Florida lay brothers were 'hopelessly drunk'. They were ordered to travel on foot to the nearest harbour from where they sailed, and then continued on foot once more to Clairvaux.

It would appear that drinking among lay brothers was quite a common occurrence, as, following the incident at Strata Florida, beer was banned from the granges of all monasteries in Wales. Even after the dissolution of the monasteries, and the attempt by the Norman conquerors to popularise wine, the common people in Wales remained faithful to beer. Nevertheless, Monastic or Trappist beer or ale is now almost entirely confined to Belgium and Holland, where six centres are still operating.

Numerous pubs are associated with pilgrims visiting various abbeys, as Myrddin ap Dafydd notes in *Enwau Tafarnau Cymru* (Welsh Pub Names). Many such inns, on routes to Ynys Enlli (Bardsey Island) and Tyddewi (St David's), have survived. Y Gegin Fawr in Aberdaron is today a café and shop, but it was there that pilgrims would wait for the boat from Porth Meudwy to ferry them across to Enlli. The hospice for sick pilgrims at Rhyd y Clafdy is still noted on the inn sign at Tu-hwnt-i'r-afon. The Saint Beuno Inn at Clynnog Fawr reflects another such association.

Other taverns in Wales have monastic connections, such as The Mynach in Cribyn, The Church Tavern in Merthyr and The Angel, next to the church at Monmouth. Cross Keys, a common inn or pub name, has connections with Saint Peter, and The Lamb at Llangeler, like various 'Lamb and Flags', was named after Agnus Dei, meaning the Lamb of God. The Saracen's Head is a name that goes back to the days of the Crusades, and pubs named The Seven Stars refer to the stars in Mary's crown. Later, this symbol was adopted by the Freemasons.

Inn and tavern names such as The Cross or The Cross Inn have obvious religious connotations and mark the former location of crosses. Although many are also sited on crossroads, it is likely that they were named after the crosses that were often raised in such places for the comfort of pilgrims.

Centuries ago, many inns belonged to churches, and these churches, like the abbeys, brewed their own ale. Indeed, the tithe laws were used in such circumstances to secure grain for the purpose of brewing. For example, The Lamb in Cardigan belonged to St Mary's Church and originally stood by the church gates.

These church inns were also places where courts of law and meetings for rent and tithe payments were held. Many staunch church members boasted the fact that the church brewed light ale, because it protected people from the evils of mead. The proximity of inns to churches indicates the connection that once existed between the two. At Llaneilian, near Colwyn Bay, the cemetery and inn share a common wall and it is impossible to enter the cemetery gate without crossing the inn's threshold.

At Ysbyty Ifan and Llangybi, two inns that are now closed are positioned opposite their corresponding churches. At Llangybi, worshipers used drink in the saddle before going to church and there was a hole in the inn's outer wall to allow them to return their empty tankards from horseback.

'Llan', the Welsh word for church, is still retained in many inn names such as Penlan Fawr, Pwllheli; Penylan, Aberaman; Penlan Oleu, Llanychâr,

The Cross Keys, Ochr y Penrhyn (Penrhyn-side near Llandudno) – symbol of Saint Peter. Inns bearing the name date back to the Reformation. This inn recalls the influence of the Catholics of nearby Neuadd y Penrhyn, who supported an illegal printing at the end of the sixteenth century.

and Tŷ'n Llan in Llandrillo. The 'Llan' used to include not just the church but also the surrounding buildings where there would often be a shop, inn and workshops, and where even boxing matches and cock-fighting would be held. Patches of land near churches and inns at Llanystumdwy and Llanarmon are known as Maes y Gwaed (The Field of Blood).

At Llanwynno, between Pontypridd and the Rhondda, the only buildings in the actual 'Llan' are the church (where fabled runner Guto Nyth Brân is buried) and The Brynffynnon. Even the various religious revivals initially did little to interfere with the old order. Itinerant preachers would be allowed ale allowances at monthly meetings. The Lamb at Rhaeader was referred to as 'the preachers' inn', as travelling preachers were welcomed there. Indeed, some religious meetings were held inside such inns. In Bangor, the very first society meeting (seiat) where nonconformists would meet to pray was held at The Virgin Tavern, (now renamed The Albion). The Sunday School at Porthcawl was held at The Victoria. The Baptist journal *Y Bedyddiwr* was printed in the cellar of The Halfway Inn at Pontllan-fraith, and Thomas Charles of Bala preached at The Prince of Wales in Tremadog.

Breakaway Methodists at Blaenau Ffestiniog were persecuted to such a degree that they would meet in secret in a tavern. In some areas, taverns became chapels. Tŷ Newydd at Abersoch was registered as a tavern in 1672. The same thing happened at The Star at Bwlch-y-groes in

Llanerchaeron Mansion in the Aeron valley, where a brew house still stands .

Pembrokeshire. One of Wales' greatest preachers, the giant of Welsh Baptism, Christmas Evans, preached at The Lewis Arms in Cardiff in 1827.

In the meantime, brewing continued in the home. In the fifteenth century, the practice was an unremarkable and common occurrence, as natural as baking bread or roasting beef. Like any task related to the household, brewing was seen as women's work. Ale was not brewed just as a means of getting merry – on the contrary, it was a way of making a safe drink. Water, after all, was full of harmful bacteria, while tea was more expensive than beer.

This home brew was weak, and was known as Penny Beer, as a gallon could be bought for a penny. It was also known as Cwrw Bach (Small Beer) and was no stronger than 2% or, at most, 2.5% alcohol, so that even children and pregnant women found it safe to drink. There was a stronger beer, which was brewed for special occasions such as farm auctions. In England this was referred to as Pudding Beer, as it contained herbs and spices such as pepper, garlic, peony and fennel. Despite its strength and its accentuated taste, this Pudding Beer was still inferior in strength and taste to Welsh Beer.

As taverns began to brew their own beer, so the custom of home brewing declined. The decline became more pronounced as commercial breweries began to appear in the eighteenth century, but home brewing survived in areas of Pembrokeshire and Carmarthenshire well into the twentieth century.

This method of home brewing, or 'macsu', was not simply a means of producing beer: it was also a means of promoting a good relationship between master and servant. It was seen as a harmless and benign bribe to persuade servants to work harder. Farms grew their own barley for brewing. Some farms also began growing hops, especially in Dyfed. Before the adoption of the Agricultural Bill in 1821, farmers would use local breweries for drying their own corn, but after 1821, the new Bill meant that the breweries' private stock had to be kept apart from that of the farmers.

One of the main areas for growing hops was the Aeron Valley in Ceredigion. Llanerchaeron, the local big estate, had its own brew house where small beer was brewed. In *Llanerchaeron: a Tale of Ten Generations, 1634-1989*, Mair Lloyd Evans analyses the mansion's brewing records. For the 6th of May 1809, the records note that malt for brewing supplied by a Jane Pugh of Aberystwyth had cost £2-2-0, while Mr Rowland Parry received £0-1-10$^{1}/_{2}$ for hops, and an unknown woman was paid £0-2-6 for brewing. On the 31st of January 1819, 'R Price Hop Merch' of Southwark received payment for hops of £12 per pocket (a sack used as a rough measure). In July 1819, Daniel Williams received £5 for malt. On the 25th of March 1834, Edward Evans of the Belle Vue, Aberystwyth paid Messers Evans and Stokes the sum of £14-6-6 for the pocket of hops purchased the previous year, while on the 10th of February 1842, Evan Lloyd was paid the sum of £43-4-0 for malt and hops sold the previous year to 'Llanairon'.

Mair Lloyd Evans estimates that it would have taken four pounds of hops to make a barrel of beer. A pocket of hops, equal to 104 lbs, cost £3-12-6 on 13th June 1776. Hops therefore sold at eight pence a pound. One pocket of hops was sufficient for twenty-six barrels, each of which held thirty-six gallons. Therefore 936 gallons, or 7,488 pints, could be made from one pocket of hops.

Brewing during the nineteenth century knew no social boundaries. Beer appealed to peasants, tenant farmers and gentry alike. The poor cottager would brew on his own hearth, and the rich landlord would brew in his mansion but would employ experts to carry out the work. Indeed, on some estates and large farms the landlord would use a purpose-built brewery. The resources would be used by both the landlord and his tenants. In some instances, certain dates were allotted for brewing in the same way that a fixed date would be allocated for sheep shearing.

Home brewing remained popular, so much so that the emerging larger breweries pressurised the government into cutting down on the numbers of private brewers. In 1878, a farmer from Llanboidy was fined £12 for brewing beer for his daughter's wedding.

Pressure was exerted not only by the government and the large breweries but also by the temperance movement. The temperance movement, which flourished throughout the religious revivals between 1859 and 1904, had a detrimental effect on home brewing. J. Geraint Jenkins observes:

> In rural Wales, temperance sprang from the experience of the eighteenth-century Methodist Revival, whose leaders taught the people to sacrifice all worldly pleasures and desires to seek the spiritual ideal. The nineteenth century, its revivals and puritanical outlook on ethical and sexual problems, strengthened and deepened the austere pattern laid down by the early Methodist leaders. Until recently in many parts of Wales, total abstinence from alcoholic drink was regarded as the kingpin of correct social behaviour; until recently too, Calvinistic Methodism, the most widespread of Welsh denominational affiliations, still required an affirmation of total abstinence from all its newly elected elders.

Nevertheless, home brewing survived in some areas – especially in west Wales and in the Gwaun valley in Pembrokeshire. Jenkins mentions ten maltsters in Haverfordwest and eight in Pembroke in 1870. The art of brewing also continued on a number of farms. Not only did farmers brew for their own and their servants' needs, but they also brewed for the community on special occasions. They would be especially busy before a family wedding. Mair Lloyd Evans describes wedding celebrations held at Llanerchaeron in 1842. As part of the festivities, beer worth £2 was distributed among the haymakers. This, she claims, paid for 120 pints of ale from a local inn, but if the beer had been brewed in the mansion's own brewhouse, it would have been an even larger quantity.

A servant girl's proficiency in brewing, at Llanerchaeron or at any such big house, would put her in good stead with a prospective employer. While home brewing declined in other parts of Wales, well into the last century it was still practised in these areas on special occasions, such as at harvest gathering.

This craft of home brewing, practised by farmer and peasant alike, varied from area to area but shared a common formula and method. One of the main necessities was a large copper pan placed on a tripod, in which water and wheat would be boiled. Later the pan was succeeded by a large electric boiler. Usually, some twelve gallons of water would be used, and after the initial boiling, the liquid would be poured into a wooden vat. A sprig of gorse or a bunch of wheat straw would be placed at the bottom of the vat, held in place by a wooden fork. This would act

*Preparing home-made malt – a series of
photographs from farmhouses in
Carmarthenshire in the 1960s*

as a strainer.

The most important ingredient in the brewing was malt. The malting would usually take place in winter. The barley was steeped in water for five days, and was then drained and spread evenly on the floor of the malthouse. It would be left for up to forty-eight hours, depending on the temperature, until minute roots emerged from the base of the grain. The barley was then regularly and carefully turned with wooden shovels and rakes. To avoid any damage to the grain, all those involved had to be barefoot. The process lasted for ten days and occasionally water was sprayed over the barley to keep it moist. The green malt was then taken to the kiln, which was heated. Here the malt was carefully dried. The heating put an end to growth and gave the malt a taste not unlike that of biscuits.

In his pamphlet on home brewing in Dyfed, Elwyn Scourfield includes a typical recipe for home brew. Two bushels of malt was placed in boiling water and this was added bucketful by bucketful to the water already in the vat. Then the vat would be covered so that the taste would be preserved and so that the beer would not escape as steam. Some ten gallons of the contents would be removed from the vat, without disturbing the settled ingredients, and this would be boiled again. The vat would then be emptied of the mash and washed clean. To the second boiling would be added a half pound of hops and six pounds of sugar. For a dark beer, brown sugar would be used. After it was brought to the boil, the contents would be strained and then poured back into the vat, where it would be allowed to cool to blood temperature before yeast was added. The vat would be covered with a blanket or an old coat for some three hours. Then it would be left for a week to give the yeast time to ferment.

The surface needed to be skimmed three times a day for three days, and more often if the need arose. In a week, the beer was ready to be poured into earthenware pots or bottles, where it would be left again for a few days before consumption.

The methods and recipes varied, as did the strength of the beer. Usually, the servants would have to make do with weak beer. This would be considerably weaker than the beer brewed for Christmas, the New Year, ploughing matches, pig-slaughter days, threshing days or wedding feasts. Christmas beer, in particular, would be strong and would be made with eight or nine gallons of water for every bushel of malt. For the weaker brew, some fourteen or fifteen gallons of water was used.

In some areas, before ploughing began, the plough would be carried into the house and blessed by throwing a few drops of the ale over it. Brewings for lesser occasions would be appropriately named according to the event. Beer brewed for re-banding cart wheels would be called banding beer (cwrw bando). Beer brewed for the completion of raising roof beams would be known as truss beer (cwrw cyplau), while beer brewed for a farm sale would be known as auction beer (cwrw acshon). The auction beer would be strong in order to enhance and quicken the bidding.

There was even a funeral beer (cwrw cynhebrwng). As in Ireland during wakes and funerals, home brew would be handed out to mourners before and after a funeral. The bearers, in particular, would receive a substantial share. In other areas, mourners would contribute money towards the wake before they left the cemetery. This would be referred to as 'arian rhaw' (spade money), because it was sometimes collected on a shovel that was held over the open grave by the clerk. The wake was then held at the nearest public house. This continued at places such as Mallwyd and Llanymawddwy until around 1830. It was known as the 'shot', and attending the 'shot' was obligatory. The men would contribute anything from sixpence to a shilling and the women would give half. Should the money run out, a cry of 'Y mae'r tŷ yn rhydd!' (this house is free!) would be raised, and another whip-round would ensue.

As in today's more sophisticated wine parties, those who attended special occasions would bring their home brew with them. This was referred to as 'ffetshin', the Welsh for 'fetching'.

Sadly, as a result of government intervention and the influence of the temperance movement, the traditions disappeared. Despite this, beer is still brewed in the old-fashioned way in areas around the Preselau and west Carmarthenshire, especially when the New Year of the old calendar (Hen Galan) is celebrated on the 13th of January.

Tafarn Bessie – Bessie's tavern – at Cwm Gwaun. The valley is the home of the 'macsu' or home brew in Pembrokeshire.

Chapter 3

Our Very Own

It was the proud boast of Eirwyn Pontshân, President of the Welsh Union of Tipplers (Undeb y Tancwyr), that even Welsh milk was better than English beer. Every time he glimpsed a brewery truck delivering Welsh beer he would reverentially doff his white cap and hail the sacred haulage as 'Cwrw Ni', or 'Our Beer' – Our Very Own.

Today, Our Very Own is limited to two big breweries and a dozen or so micro breweries, but it still exists, despite the greed of the huge conglomerates that threaten to swallow not only our beer but its makers as well.

Welsh beer or ale nowadays can mean any type of ale or beer brewed in Wales. But Welsh ale really did exist, not as a geographical term but as a drink that boasted its very own recipe and character. Even after the recipe was stolen by invaders, it remained Welsh ale.

The creation of mead could have occurred accidentally and so could wine: different fruits contain their own sugars and yeasts. Grapes, for example, can ferment after they have been pressed, creating a quite drinkable form of wine, but beer is probably a different matter. In order for beer to be brewed, barley needs to be turned to malt and mixed with boiling water and yeast to form an alcoholic drink. This is not as simple as it sounds. It is a sophisticated method that goes back to 4,000 BC in the Middle East. It was probably the Egyptians who first grew barley specifically for brewing purposes, and Babylon soon followed. It is said that the god of wine, Dionysus, fled from Mesopotamia because of his hatred for the beer that was brewed there. Personally, I believe he left because of the natives' practice of drinking beer through a straw. Ancient illustrations portray them doing just that, the sissies.

In what is referred to in the Old Testament as Ur of Chaldea, half the harvested yield was earmarked for brewing. Brewing was a task performed under the patronage of the goddess of cooking, Ninkasi. In Ur in around 1,750 BC, King Hammurabi made the first known law prohibiting beer that was too weak and too expensive. In Ancient Egypt, brewing guidelines were formulated by none other than Osiris himself, god of life and resurrection. The finished brew was called *zythum*.

Despite the complexity of the brewing process, it is possible that a primitive form of fermentation was discovered through an accident of nature, as was probably the case with mead. Imagine some Neolithic

Eirwyn Pontshân, President of the Welsh Union of Tipplers

baker kneading dough. He or she discovers that partly baked dough made from germinating dry seeds tended to be better preserved. The next step might have been for the bread to be crumbled and steeped in water. Then the liquid might have been filtered and drunk. And bingo: people started falling over.

Journalists have always been known for their propensity for drink, and it may be no coincidence that grain and journalism are closely connected. When humans discovered the art of writing, somewhere around the Uruk area of Mesopotamia – today known as Iraq – the first printing presses consisted of pebbles and sea shells being pressed into a bed of clay to form messages. These early marks were used to denote the state of the grain crops. As grain is closely associated with brewing, many of these prehistoric hacks may have been among the world's earliest alcoholic drinkers.

The Thracians are credited with bringing brewing to Europe, with the Greeks close behind them. The Thracians brewed an alcoholic drink known as *Bryton*. Before you could say Eureka, we in Wales were following suit. Here we have an old and honoured brewing tradition. Long before any mention was made of English beer, King Ine of Wessex formulated laws around 690 which included a list of pricing guidelines for the purchase of land. Tracts of land were measured in plots of sixty acres, large enough to support an ordinary-sized family and its dependents. An area consisting of ten such plots was equal to ten vats of honey, three hundred loaves, twelve ambers of Welsh ale, thirty ambers of clear ale, two cows or ten wethers, ten geese, twenty hens, ten cheeses, a full amber of butter, five trout, twenty pounds of feed or one hundred eels. These statistics indicate that twelve measures of Welsh ale was worth two-and-a-half times that of clear ale, even if the picture is clouded somewhat by the fact that no one now seems to know the meaning of 'amber' in such a context. The word occurs twice in the Domesday Book but with no explanation of the size or amount.

By the reign of King Alfred (849-899) ale and ale houses were common throughout Britain (now we know why old Alfred incinerated his cakes). But Welsh ale was still the best. In 901, as part of an annual payment to King Edward for leasing land, the Bishop of Winchester, Denewulf, was requested to make twelve sesters, or 364 ounces of sweet Welsh ale. It was probably sweetened with honey. Indeed, some agreements insisted on such a clause.

In the twelfth century, Abbot Medeshamstede exchanged the Sempringham estate with one of his tenants for an annual payment of a horse, thirty shillings and one day's work, as well as fifteen mittans of clear ale, five mittans of Welsh ale, or fifteen sesters – 430 ounces – of mild ale. Again it is not clear what a 'mittan' amounted to, but it is clear that Welsh ale was three times the value of clear ale, which was, presumably, English. Sempringham Abbey was where Princess Gwenllian (1282-1337), daughter of Prince Llywelyn, the Last Prince of Wales, was exiled to become a nun. It is quite possible, therefore, that during her exile she could have tasted the ale of her native land.

It should be noted that Welsh beer did not necessarily have to originate in Wales. It was the ingredients that determined whether it was Welsh ale or not. Welsh ale was unique and was brewed before the Saxons drove the indigenous population westwards. Much as the Saxons hated its brewers, they simply loved Welsh ale, so much so that they stole the recipe.

In the eighth century, Offa, that well-known pre-JCB dyke-builder, presented lands to Worcester Cathedral in lieu of a payment that included sixteen quarts of Welsh ale. It is known that beer during this period was divided into three classifications – clear, light and Welsh. Evidently, Welsh ale was neither clear nor light so, presumably, it was strong and heavy. It also contained spices such as cinnamon, cloves and ginger. According to one law, Welsh ale was itself sub-divided into common ale and spicy ale. One barrel of mead was equivalent to two casks of spicy ale or four barrels of common ale.

Hywel Dda (Hywel the Good), who died around 950, formulated a system of native Welsh laws that included edicts on ale. The laws named two kinds of beer: *Braggot*, which was paid to a king as a tribute when the donor was made a Freeman of a town or city, and *Cwrwf*, or *Cwrw*, which is still the Welsh word for beer. The recipe for Braggot has survived. Malted barley was added to boiling water along with honey, cinnamon, cloves, ginger, pepper and various kinds of reeds.

The death knell for Welsh ale was sounded when a new law was passed requiring that the contents of ale should be limited to malt, yeast and water. Nevertheless, what is referred to as Welsh ale is still brewed in various parts of the world. Ironically, the ale brewed by the Saint Louis Brewery in the USA which is advertised as Welsh ale is listed as English Pale Ale in the company's brochures.

Brewing may have suffered a decline, but home brew enjoyed a renaissance during the 1980s when beer kits proved to be very popular. Home brewers were fettered, however, by the guidelines set down by the companies producing the kits. Very few home-brewers continued using their own traditional recipes. Alan and Brenda Jones of Aberlleinau, Pentrecagal near Newcastle Emlyn are exceptions. They still brew in the ways of the traditional south west Wales home brewers. The craft has

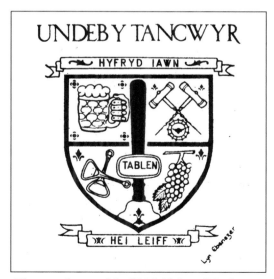

The coat of arms of the Welsh Union of Tipplers

29

Harris Thomas, composer of the Union of Tipplers' anthem. He is seen with a portrait of the Vicar of Penstwffwl, painted by Victor Neep.

been inherited on both sides of the family. The contents of their brew are all natural: malt, water, yeast, sugar and hops – or nettles if hops are scarce. A sprig of gorse is placed at the bottom of the brewing vat to act as a strainer.

To the Joneses, the calendar rules the brewing: one brewing takes a week, and the brew is then left to mature for several more weeks. The old farming calendar does not exist any more, so the Joneses brew for events such as the Royal Welsh Show – not to enter in any competition but for drinking in the caravan at Llanelwedd. The Jones' beer has amazing qualities, as I can readily testify. Alan insists that an incomer to the area who found it difficult to learn Welsh drank some of Aberlleinau's home brew one night, and soon afterwards could speak Welsh perfectly!

Is Alan worried that some unscrupulous visitor might take away his recipe? 'I have no worries on that score', he says. 'After three pints, none will be able to remember a thing. I've known some visitors, after three pints, having to sleep in their wellington boots because they are too drunk to take them off.'

Alan has exhibited his craft at the National History Museum at St Fagans. Among his many types of beers there is a spiced beer, which harks back to where this chapter started: with Welsh ale.

Welsh ale is also celebrated by the Welsh Union of Tipplers. Members of the original Union still survive although the movement has no known organisation. It was formed at the Aberystwyth National Eisteddfod in 1952, when Eirwyn Pontshân, one of our greatest raconteurs, was elected Life President. Its proud boast is that it is the only trade union not ever to contemplate taking strike action. It has its own anthem, composed by architect Harris Thomas of Caernarfon, and later it created its own banner and coat of arms.

The anthem encapsulates many of the stories and characters referred to by the President in his various addresses. This is a loose translation:

> There are wondrous things in store
> For the drinkers of the Boar
> When Walter Pantybarlat's on the spree,
> Are you ready, Mrs Morgan?
> The Sais will play the organ,
> Well now then, all together – one, two, three.
>
> Chorus:
> High life is the song when Eirwyn comes along,
> Cymru's tipple is the best on land or sea,

And Penstwffwl's genial Vicar will pay for all our liquor,
Union of Tipplers all are we.

What if Mari keeps the jam
Beneath the baby in the pram,
What if Ned and Madam Patti are in heaven?
That old sun will wake the seeds,
If we can't have flowers, we'll take the weeds,
And we'll drink and fill our needs till past eleven.

Chorus

No one needs to pay the bill,
Let's all sing and drink our fill
With Pantycelyn's student till stop tap;
If the binder's in the muck,
The Inspector's in his truck
With that great king of the farmyard on his lap.

Chorus

The words are obviously cryptic, yet every line tells a story, a story that is never to be revealed by the members. Those who break the sacred oath are condemned to a life sentence of drinking water. The ultimate punishment for persistent offenders is to be sentenced to drink English beer.

Part of the exhibition at the New Quay Honey Farm

A traditional beehive

The mead house

A selection of meads at the farm

www.thehoneyfarm.co.uk

Alan Jones, Pentrecagal – a master home-brewer at work

34

Houses bearing the name 'Bragdy' (Brewhouse) such as this one at Dolgellau are to be found throughout Wales.

Tafarn y Bedol (The Horseshoe Inn) in Dyffryn Conwy, indicating the connection between beer and work. The inn stands on the old drovers' route.

Brains – the national beer

www.sabrain.com

Felinfoel, one of only two large breweries left in Wales

www.felinfoel-brewery.com

One of the few Buckley signs left today

The lager has disappeared from Wrexham

Old cider mills at the National History Museum, St Fagan's

Stalls promoting Welsh cider at the national agricultural show at Builth Wells

Welsh Cider Society: www.welshcider.co.uk

An advert for Fron-goch whisky and one of the few bottles that has survived

An old Fron-goch whisky advert

Penderyn Whisky's distillery today

www.welsh-whisky.co.uk

Evan Evans, Simon Buckley's brewery at Llandeilo
www.evan-evans.com

46

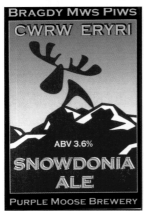

Products from some of Wales' smaller breweries

Chapter 4

King Arthur

The most famous alcoholic drink in the world is probably Guinness. Many a Welsh rugby supporter on a biennial visit to Dublin has been undone by Arthur Guinness' black stuff, and what self-respecting Irishman did not gargle on Guinness while relaxing from building dams or laying that other black stuff on Wales' roads around the middle of the last century, when work was scarce in the old country?

Apart from such occasional connections, what has Guinness to do with Wales? Quite a lot, in fact. It has been claimed that it was a Welshman who invented the drink, and had there not been a U-turn by the government of the day in the eighteenth century, it would have had much stronger Welsh connections. Indeed, had the government not made a rare sympathetic move on behalf of the Irish, Guinness would have been a Welsh drink.

Records of alcoholic drink in Ireland go back to at least 1 AD, when the Greek physician Disocorides referred to the Hiberni, or the Irish (and to

Wil Sam, contemplating a drop of the Black Stuff

the Britons in general) brewing a drink called 'courmi', the name for beer. In Old Irish it was known as 'coirm'. In 438 AD, Senchus Mor, the Book of Ancient Irish Laws, refers to the growing of barley for brewing purposes. Indeed, it is alleged that Saint Patrick himself had a brewer among his retinue, a man called Mescan, while Saint Bridget is also said to have brewed ale for the church at Eastertide.

In Dublin, ale was brewed on the banks of the Poddle river by 1300, and by 1610 there were 1,180 alehouses and 91 brewing houses in the city. Arthur Guinness was therefore one in a long line of a thriving tradition.

Arthur should be placed in context here. In the eighteenth century, large breweries were being set up in England. Naturally, this was peculiar to the growing towns and cities where a large part of the population lived. Another reason for locating breweries in the larger towns was the poor condition of the roads. Transporting goods was difficult, so the breweries were established where the demand was greatest.

The earliest developments were seen in London, with companies such as Whitbread and Truman leading the way. An anonymous official history of Guinness, published in 1939, explains the situation in London at the time. It was around 1722 that a dark beer was produced there, which combined the flavour and general qualities of a mixture of heavy, sweet ale with a lighter, bitter beer. Its chief patrons were the labouring classes, particularly porters, and it became known as Porter. In contrast, the predominant beer brewed in Dublin was a brown beer. There was no Porter, even though it was, by then, London's most popular tipple.

The first reference to porter being brewed in Dublin is found in a Petition presented in 1736 to the House of Commons by Joseph and Ephraim Thwaites, who requested assistance in promoting the brewing of Irish Porter, which had 'been brought to perfection after repeated and expensive experiments'.

Brewers producing porter, or stout, were able to export their product to Ireland much more cheaply than the Irish themselves could produce and sell. In Ireland the tolls imposed by England were seen as unjust, so when Arthur Guinness' brewery opened in 1759 at St James' Gate in Dublin, the great man also began to look elsewhere. Guinness' anonymous history reveals how close the brewery came to moving, lock, stock and porter-barrel to Wales, citing the report to the Irish House of Commons of a committee which was appointed in 1773 to consider a petition from the Corporation of Brewers:

It came out in evidence that the duty paid in Ireland on imported Porter was only a small fraction of one shilling per barrel, which compared with the duty of nearly 5s 6d per barrel on the Irish brew, placed Dublin firms at a hopeless disadvantage.

Among the witnesses examined before this committee was Mr. Arthur Guinness, founder of the firms of Arthur Guinness & Co. He confirmed the evidence of Mr. George Thwaites, Master of the Brewers' Corporation, who said that when he began business 34 years before, there were 70 breweries in Dublin, whereas now there were only about 30. Mr. Guinness said that he had been a brewer for about 17 or 18 years, that the trade had gradually declined since about 1759, and that he intended to set up a brewery at Carnarvon [sic] or Holyhead if he could find a brewery ready built there.

In around 1777 the Government relented on the matter of Excise Duty and

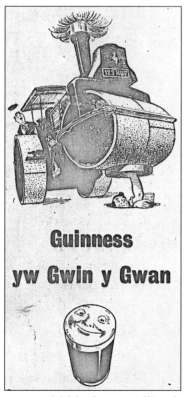

Welsh adverts extolling the virtue of Guinness in the 1950s

this resulted in a significant downturn in the amount of porter exported to Ireland.

By 1816, Irish porter was being exported. The drink was sold under the guise of being medicinal. It was reputed to cure insomnia, weariness, constipation and nervous disorders. Around 1782, Henry Grattan, MP, a barrister and Irish nationalist, wrote to Arthur Guinness stating that he regarded the brewery as 'the actual nurse of the people, and entitled to every encouragement, favour and exemption', and a Cavalry Officer, who was wounded in Belgium after the Battle of Waterloo, wrote in his diary that he found Guinness porter to be of great benefit in restoring health and strength.

Guinness has always led the field in advertising. During its first advertising campaign in journals, papers and on posters, Welsh-language adverts quickly appeared. 'Guinness yw Gwin y Gwan' (Guinness is the

Wine of the Weak) became a household jingle in Wales as did 'Cato Pawb! Fy Nguinness i' (My Goodness, my Guinness!) Yes, in Welsh, Guinness even mutated!

It should be noted that the tradition that Guinness is brewed using Liffey water is a fallacy. Neither is it true that water from a well at St James' Gate was used. A well does exist there, but its water was used exclusively for cleaning the plant and equipment, and for cooling the product. The water used for brewing comes from the same wells in County Kildare that feed the upper reaches of the Grand Canal. Apart from water, the other basic ingredients are malt, hops and yeast.

What of the claim that the recipe for Guinness was created by a Welshman? One individual who believe this was Timothy Lewis, who contributed a feature to *Y Ford Gron* (The Round Table) in April 1933, recalling his time as a soldier in Ireland in 1915. During his service he visited Cashell Abbey where he had an interesting conversation with one of the keepers. According to him, the last Protestant Bishop of Cashell was a man called Price from the Vale of Glamorgan. He became famous for his hospitality and for the standard and strength of his drink, and when he died he left behind its recipe in a communion letter. It is alleged that it was this recipe that was later used to brew Guinness.

This story has been confirmed by author T. Llew Jones. In a letter to the Welsh folk magazine *Llafar Gwlad* he states that this Bishop Price was of the same lineage as the Prices of Rhydcolomennod (Pigeonsford) near Llangrannog. This is in turn reiterated in the book *Llangrannog and the Pigeonsford Family* by Evelyn Hope. Price was one of a number of the sons of the Rhydycolomennod family who became bishops over a number of years. Some of these attended Dublin University and then went on to serve in Ireland.

This member of the Price family, Arthur, who became Bishop of Cashell, tarnished his good name for taking off the abbey roof as a protest against Catholics who still worshipped there. T. Llew Jones notes:

> But long before he was promoted Bishop and Archbishop (indeed, when he was a rector), Price had recruited a servant, Richard Guinness. Richard was a common Protestant, born around 1690 near a place called Cellbridge. He was known as 'Stewart and agent to ... the rector Rev Arthur Price'.

According to Jones, when this Richard Guinness became a father, his son was named Arthur as a token of respect for his employer, Arthur Price, and Price accepted the invitation to become the child's Godfather. Price had by now become famous for 'the quality of the "black beer" with which he was wont to regale his guests … '

It was Richard Guinness who would organise the seasonal brewing at the Archbishop's Palace, overseeing the making of a drink that was described as 'a brew of a very palatable nature'. This, claims Jones, is proof that the recipe for brewing the 'black beer' arrived at the Archbishop's Palace with the servant, or that it had belonged to the priest for some time but Guinness had discovered a more effective way of brewing. When the young Arthur Guinness reached adulthood he took over the brewing duties from his father. He was in great demand among powerful friends of the Archbishop, and many powerful dignitaries thronged to the Palace to taste the drink. Arthur went on to open his first brewery in 1756 with the aid of a sum of £100 given to him by Arthur Price. This lends some credibility to the story, and strengthens the connection between Wales and the Black Stuff.

However, another version of the story accuses Arthur Guinness of stealing the recipe from Wales. Tradition maintains that, whilst travelling regularly between Dublin and London, the great man chanced upon a particular kind of porter at an ale house in Llanfairfechan, a village on the stagecoach route between Holyhead and London. It is said that the brew pleased him so much that he went home and recreated it in Dublin. At least two ale houses existed in the area at the time: Llety (Hostelry) and Gwyndy (White House). However, the imagination is stretched somewhat by the allegation that Gwyndy should be Gwin Du (Black Wine).

However, at least three sites in the area were used for malting, and this lends some credibility to the story. Why the need for so many in such a small place? Was malt from Llanfairfechan exported to Dublin? Unlike Guinness, the theft version of the story is difficult to swallow.

What of the allegation that the Guinness served in Ireland is better, stronger and of a superior taste to that which is sold in the UK? That is another myth. It is a matter of caring. The better it is cared for, the better Guinness is to the taste. It is also true that the more Guinness that is passed through the pump, the better the taste. Guinness must be kept flowing. That should be no problem at all.

Chapter 5

Iron, Coal and Ale

Where there's industry, there are people, and where there are people, their needs must be catered for. Among those needs is the need for relaxation and a drink or two after work. The bigger the population, the larger the thirst, and so the first big breweries were built in the heavily populated industrial areas.

In England, this meant London. It was in London that large brewing companies such as Whitbread and Truman established their breweries. Such breweries were conspicuously absent from Wales until the nineteenth century, but there was one exception.

It was the copper industry that attracted the Cambrian Porter Brewery to Swansea, following Phillips and Kendall's successful application to build a brewery on the Strand in 1792. Soon another sprang up nearby, opened by Edward Davies. Both businesses, however, were short-lived. The records of the Cambrian Porter Brewery reveal that the business changed hands no less than six times within a quarter of a century. After Phillips and Kendall came William Shepherd, Henry Bonham, Samuel Hawkins and George Hayes, all of them London businesses, and by 1822 it was being run by Haynes and Morgan. Little is known of Edward Davies, the only competitor, but by the middle of the century, both breweries had closed. Nevertheless, the drought did not last for long. Soon George Rolls opened a brewery at Meysydd, which he named the Swansea Old Brewery.

The growth of breweries through south-western Wales was a slow and gradual process. It was in 1799 that the first brewery was opened in Llanelli. This forerunner of Buckleys was established by Henry Childs. In north Wales, the first Wrexham brewery opened in the same year.

In south Wales, however, the emerging coal and iron industries soon opened the door for brewers. The first area to be industrialised was mid Glamorgan, in around the middle of the eighteenth century. This industrialisation rapidly opened up commercial opportunities and, naturally, recreational needs followed. The iron industry, in particular, was thirsty work – especially so for the furnace workers. The brewers spotted their opportunity almost immediately. Despite the attempts of some owners and of the temperance movement to prohibit alcohol or at least persuade workers not to succumb to the devil's drink, Dowlais became one of the biggest drinking towns in Wales, despite the fact that the unemployment rate at one time was seventy percent.

Hitherto, the brewers' greatest problem had been transport and haulage, but now, with the heads of the Valleys having been opened up by industrialists such as John Guest at Dowlais and Richard Crawshay at Cyfarthfa, the roads, railways and canals, built for transporting coal and iron and steel, were just as useful for transporting beer. Later, these amenities would become a hindrance. After all, if these roads, railroads and canals made it easier to transport beer from place to place *within* Wales, they would, in time, be just as useful for transporting beer *into* Wales from England.

The attitude to drinking on the part of the iron and steel barons was most ambiguous. While some workers were issued with beer tokens as an incentive to work harder, John Guest of the Dowlais Steel Company announced in 1831 that he would not employ anyone who kept a pub. Indeed, he went as far as to close numerous public houses in the vicinity of the steelworks, and he hired lawyers to oppose applications for opening new pubs in the area.

Despite this resistance, Merthyr was the first town to witness the after-effects of the new brewing industrial developments. At that time, Merthyr was the most populous town in Wales, with a population three times larger than Cardiff. The first brewery of any note to be opened in Merthyr was Williams and Bryant in 1830. In less than twenty years there were ten breweries. By 1871, there were fourteen breweries and 180 pubs.

After Williams and Bryant, one of the first breweries in the area was opened on a site by the Brecon Road by Watkin Davies. It was named the Merthyr Brewery and was soon swallowed by Giles and Harrap, which specialised in brewing mild and bitter beer as well as stout. Giles and Harrap also specialised in fine wines and spirits and owned outlets in England, Ireland and Scotland. Such were the profits, that Harrap provided a leisure park for use by its workers, tenants and their families.

Another important brewery was the Taff Vale, opened by Thomas Evans during the 1840s. It was bought by David Williams in 1867. In 1904 – the year of Evan Roberts' great religious revival – the brewery was completely rebuilt. When it was eventually bought by the Rhymney Brewery in 1936 it owned twenty-five leasehold pubs. Within three years it owned 362 pubs and hotels.

The Pontycapel Brewery was opened at Cefn Coed and it also set up a number of pubs in Cefn Coed as well as in Merthyr and Dowlais. It was mentioned by Alfred Barnard in *Noted Breweries of Great Britain and Ireland*, one of only four Welsh breweries deemed worthy of inclusion by the author. It seems that he had been attracted there by a particular brew:

The Pontycapel Brewery at Cefncoedycymer, c. 1900

The old Glenview Brewery at Pontypridd, now demolished

The XXXX brew was known as 'Star Bright' – a beverage celebrated for its strength and flavour, not only throughout the South of Wales, but in the neighbouring counties of England.

This brewery had been opened by Robert Millar in the 1840s but its development is attributed to Thomas Pearce, who bought it in 1860. The plant was powered by a water mill, and water for brewing was drawn from nearby Ffynnon Oer (Cold Spring).

Smaller breweries were also opened in the area. At Cefn Coed there was the Meredith Brewery, which closed in 1920. There were others at Caedraw, and at the Clarence Hotel, kept by D. W. Huggins in Dowlais. These were comparatively small ventures, with a capacity of some thirty barrels while the Cyfarthfa Brewery, a five-storey building, could produce forty barrels at a time.

It was Bute's arrival and the establishment of his iron works at Rhymney Bridge in 1825 that led to one of the largest brewing dynasties in south Wales. Critical to the venture was Andrew Buchan, a Scotsman who was appointed manager at the company's shop, where workers could exchange wage tokens for food and drink.

Bute was responsible for building the town of Rhymney – the houses,

Views of the industrial Valleys seen on pub signs

shops, farm and church. In 1838 a brewery was added, and Buchan was employed as manager. He would later go on to establish a company under his own name. By 1867, Rhymney Brewery was producing 12,500 barrels annually and owned twenty-nine pubs.

Buchan died in 1870 and was succeeded by various chairmen. The company prospered and won prizes for its beer in Britain and on the continent. The Coronation of Edward VII was celebrated with the launching of a special brew, 'King's Ale'. The brewery continued to prosper and added to its empire by buying the old Heolgerrig Brewery in 1916.

By now, however, the tide was beginning to turn: English brewers saw an opening, and beer from England began flowing into Wales. Over the mountain at Aberdâr, three important breweries – the Trecynon, the Black Lion and the George – were bought by Alsopp.

Brewing practically ended in the area after Powell Duffryn bought the Rhymney Iron Works – which owned Rhymney Brewery – in 1920. Eventually it was bought out by Whitbreads, and brewing continued until 1978.

However, the story of the Rhymney Brewery does not quite end there. The brewery's name was resurrected and brewing began at the Pant

A full load leaving the Rock Brewery, Aberdâr

Industrial Estate in January 2005. This mini brewery concentrates on bottled and keg beer.

If the iron works' furnaces created thirst, so did coal dust, and breweries aimed at slaking the thirst of the miners sprouted up side by side with those initiated by the iron works. The main source for this market was the Ely Brewery at Cardiff, which opened in around the middle of the eighteenth century. By 1875 James Ward, who had named the venture Tower Brewery, was producing three kinds of stout, as well as bitter and a choice of mild. Immediately in front of it stood Crosswell's New Brewery.

The two breweries had contrasting backgrounds: the Ely Brewery was a wholly Welsh concern and, originally set up in 1853, was closed some thirty years later, only to be resurrected in 1877. The renowned choir conductor Caradog was one of its directors. Crosswell, a wholly English company, was not established in Cardiff till 1897, and it only lasted some forty years as an independent brewery.

James Ward bought a number of breweries and began expanding his business up the Valleys. Initially reaching Aberdâr, he later took over the Rhondda Valleys Breweries at Treherbert and Pontypridd to form the Rhondda and Ely Breweries. This opened the door to owning almost a hundred pubs in the heartland of the coalfields. Subsequently he took over the Pontypridd United Breweries, upping the number of pubs he owned to 284. Then disaster hit the brewing industry. The 1926 strike threatened the livelihood of up to ninety percent of the Rhondda's publicans. Ten years later, the Rhondda Valleys Breweries had accumulated debts of over £100,000.

There was so much wheeling and dealing between breweries, so many amalgamations, that it is almost impossible to follow them. In his classic work *The Prince of Ales* and his follow-up volume *Cardiff Pubs and Breweries*, Brian Glover details the various developments. In summary, it was the great invader Whitbread that brought most of the breweries in Cardiff – and south Wales more widely – under its umbrella.

In the meantime, at the other end of the coalfield, another brewery was established. By the middle of the nineteenth century, the Vale of Neath Brewery at Llangatwg was the largest in the area. It suffered a setback when the brewery tower was destroyed by an accidental fire. Seven years were to go by before the site was bought by local businessman Evan Evans. He had already gained wide experience in the brewing industry. One notable feather in his hat was his acquisition of the right to stock Guinness. He turned the Vale of Neath Brewery into the biggest in Wales,

The new Rhymney Brewery at Dowlais, continuing an old tradition

selling a thousand barrels of beer per week and employing two hundred staff.

Evan Evans combined brewing with mining. In partnership with his son-in-law, David Bevan, he owned four mines, a combined business that exported 800 tons of coal a day, mostly to France. Evans and Bevan went on to buy two more mines. Evan Evans had seven daughters, and he named one of his coal mines Seven Sisters after them. Around the original houses, in an area called Brick Lane, a whole village grew up, as well as three mines: the Dillwyn, or Nant-y-cafn, in 1884; Brynteg in 1885, and, later, Henllan. Like his father before him, Evan Evans was elected Mayor of Neath. After his death he was succeeded by his son-in-law, who renamed the company by combining the family names: this is how Evan Evans Bevan was formed.

David Bevan was succeeded, in turn, by his son, Martyn. Gradually, however, the family lost interest in brewing, and in 1967 the brewing business was sold to Whitbread, the company which had already bought the Rhymney Brewery. Before the bargain was sealed, signed and delivered, the brewery again suffered significant damage from a fire. In 1972, the brewery closed, and consequently 140 jobs were lost.

For over a century in industrial south Wales, iron, coal and beer had been harmonious and natural companions. Today the trio remain united: these three industries in south Wales have all but disappeared.

Chapter 6

The National Ale

Thanks to its quality and some brilliant advertising, Guinness has become one of Ireland's icons, indeed its foremost icon. The stated ambition of one of only two big breweries remaining in Wales is to repeat the success of its Irish cousin in its own country. Brains Brewery's ambition is to identify its product with the Welsh nation. Typically, in 2006 it produced a brew called 'The Land of My Fathers' to celebrate the 150th anniversary of the Welsh national anthem.

By the end of the last millennium, no beer had identified itself more with its home city or town than Brains. In essence, Brains was Cardiff and Cardiff was Brains. Producing 'The Land of My Fathers', however, was just another step on a journey that has been slowly but surely turning Brains into a national product.

Brains has sponsored various sports organisations over the years, including soccer, cricket and darts, but it was its promotion of the national rugby team that proved to be the biggest winner. Wales won the 2004-2005 Grand Slam with the players displaying the Brains logo on their shirts. To mark the promotion, the company launched a special brew called 'Bread of Heaven'. Now the brewery is well on the way to reaching its goal. In securing its exclusive sponsorship of the Welsh rugby team, Brains beat such well-known brands as Coca Cola, O2 and Orange. A recent opinion poll showed that seventy percent of those questioned thought that Brains SA was the best-known beer in Wales.

Cardiff was only a small town in 1713 when brewing began at the Old Brewery. This brewery, which would become Brains, was sited in an area of Cardiff with the best water supply, and stood above a deep well. Records show that in 1831 there was only one brewer in Cardiff, who was named James Walters. The brewery became Williams' malthouse and then passed to Frederick Prosser by 1855, and then to John Thomas, who passed it on to his sons, John Griffen Thomas and Edward Inkerman Thomas. Subsequently John became the sole owner.

Oddly enough, Brains can thank the Sunday Closing Act of 1881 for its inheritance. In *Prince of Ales* Brian Glover writes:

Agitation in favour of Sunday closing had been growing throughout Wales during the 1860s and 1870s. A Swansea conference in 1875 passed a resolution that 'a measure be introduced into Parliament specially for Wales providing for the entire closing of public houses on the Lord's Day'. Spearheaded by the Good Templars, the bandwagon began to roll. Petitions proliferated.

When the Bill was eventually passed, John Griffen Thomas saw this as a mortal blow to his business, so he sold up to his brother-in-law, Samuel Arthur Brain, who set up in business with his uncle, Joseph Benjamin Brain. The Old Brewery became Brains Brewery, and it still remains in the hands of the family. Almost immediately the two partners built new premises behind the old building, which used to stand behind The Albert in St Mary's Street. The new brewery was capable of brewing seven times more than the Old Brewery.

As a result of the Sunday Closing Act, the brewing trade hit back by producing bottled beer for take-away, and opening Working Men's Clubs, which were licensed to sell drinks on Sundays. In 1881 there was only one such club in Cardiff. By 1883 there were thirteen and three years later there were 141, with Brains supplying many of them. When the Brain family took over in 1882, the brewery owned eleven pubs. By 1900 it owned over eighty pubs and was producing fifteen hundred barrels a week.

As well as being a shrewd and astute businessman, Samuel Brain was also a public figure in local government, and in 1899 he was elected Mayor. He had by then registered the business as a limited company that was worth £350,000. When Samuel died in 1903, the business remained in the family, but this was not his only legacy. One of the company's beers, SA, was named after him. This tipple earned itself such a reputation that it became known as 'Skull Attack'.

The company decided to expand by adding various premises in different parts of Cardiff. This included taking over the Cambrian Brewery in Womanby Street. The Great War put paid temporarily to the company's reconstruction plans, but in 1919 a new brewery was opened in Nora Street, and the old buildings were demolished. By then the company was brewing a range of barrelled beer as well as bottled beer, both in the Old and New Breweries, including Red Dragon, which was to become Brains Dark. The Dark became an icon, and is still as Cardiff in character as Clarkes' Pies.

Brains, like Guinness, hardly needed advertising, but just like its Irish counterpart, it did advertise and with great success. The slogan 'It's Brains You Want' was widely seen and heard. It was taken a step further when 'Brains' in the slogan became 'BrAIns', the 'AI' signifying 'A1', or top class.

Brains' Old Brewery in 1890, with the original building on the left. The stack was a feature of Cardiff until 1978. Below, the interior.

Images of Brains Brewery

As Cardiff Docks became known throughout the world, so too did Brains. It was enjoyed by visiting sailors from every country under the sun. The company's North and South pub in the docks was famous for its landlady, a Mrs Bryant, who acted as unofficial banker for sailors departing on long voyages, looking after their money and valuables while they were away. Even today, The Packet in the rejuvenated docklands area in Cardiff Bay is still a legendary place that recalls the good old days.

Brains' empire grew to around 120 pubs, some of which, like The Old Arcade, became well known to rugby supporters worldwide. Facing Bute Street, The Golden Cross with its unique tiling was similarly familiar. The legendary boxer 'Peerless' Jim Driscoll kept a Brains pub, The Duke of Edinburgh, which has long since been pulled down.

The appearance during the 1970s of CAMRA (The Campaign For Real Ale) and its efforts to promote real ale had a positive effect on businesses such as Brains. The brewing at the Old Brewery increased by fifty percent. By the end of 1979, work on the brewery's expansion plans was completed at a cost of almost £3 million, raising the brewing capacity to eighteen million pints a year. Brains had become a Welsh oasis in a desert of English brewing.

One of Brains' great achievements was seeing off an English brewing giant whose sights were set on conquering the Welsh coalfields. Hancocks had its roots in Wiveliscombe, just across the Bristol Channel, and for a while it did indeed manage to rule the south Wales beer market, making its HB one of Wales' best-loved beers.

The Welsh coalfields proved too tempting a market for the company, and by 1871 two of Hancocks' agents, John and Joseph Gaskell – father and son – had secured a foot-hold for distributing their product at the Bute Western Dock in Cardiff. It was then a short step for the company to brew its own beer in Wales. In 1883 it bought the North and Low Brewery and its associate pubs in Cardiff Docks, and the Gaskells were made managers. A year later it bought Newport's Anchor Brewery and Hancocks then set up its official Welsh branch. William Hancock was registered in June 1887 as owning over seventy pubs in the Cardiff and Newport area.

Hancocks endeared itself to the Welsh because one of the family's sons, Frank, played rugby for Cardiff and even captained Wales. His brother Philip, on the other hand, played for Blackheath, England and the British Lions.

Hancocks' empire grew apace and by the early 1890s it owned some three hundred tied pubs, another hundred associated pubs, and was responsible for two-thirds of the beer trade in Cardiff. It produced two thousand barrels a week, and in just thirteen years it became the biggest brewing and bottling business in Wales.

The company's policy was to swallow up smaller breweries and centralise its production on one site in Cardiff. With this in mind the company bought the County Brewery in Penarth Road in 1894, but this was not enough: it went on expanding, reaching as far west as Lampeter.

During the Great War, two of Hancocks' dray horses, King and Bob, were recruited to haul the big guns, and when they returned as heroes they starred on the company's publicity posters. Another publicity stunt was to build a beer tanker, named the Flagon Wagon, which was the shape of a bottle. Neon signs were positioned across busy streets and a caricature of John Bull became the company's logo. Later, the company's Sign of Hospitality was seen throughout Wales.

Hancocks' march seemed unstoppable, as it pushed up towards Merthyr. Such was its success that it drew the attention of Bass Worthington, and a loose partnership was formed. In 1961, Hancocks' Chairman, Joseph Gaskell, was appointed to the Bass Worthington board.

By now, Hancocks had reached Aberystwyth, where it bought Roberts' Brewery. David Roberts had opened a brewery at Trefechan in 1844, situating it close to the harbour and near two wells. Along with his two sons, he formed a private company and took over three-quarters of the town's pubs. He built three of Aberystwyth's hotels: the Cambrian, the Central and the Castle. Then he took over the Facey Brewery at Abergavenny. The company now owned one hundred pubs and supplied an area stretching from Tywyn to Newtown, down to Abergavenny and across to Llandeilo and Haverfordwest.

In 1960, Hancocks bought Roberts for £680,000, thus adding 117 pubs to its empire of 440 pubs. This was the twentieth brewery that the English giant swallowed. The company did not honour its earlier promise to keep the Roberts name, however, and brewing soon ended at Aberystwyth. In Cardiff, the company grew ever larger and added the famous Barley Bright and Allbright to its range of beers.

Hancocks' dray on the road with another load on the streets of Merthyr Tydfil

Bass Worthington, already amalgamated with Bass Charrington, then bought Hancocks for £7.7 million and formed Welsh Brewers. Despite its patriotic name, business was run from Burton and London, and the name was changed to Bass Wales and West. The company then bought Ind Coope of Burton, and the Cardiff base was closed and 126 jobs were lost.

By this time, only one sign remained to connect Cardiff and Hancocks – the Allbright sign on the brewery chimney stack in Crawshay Street. That site fell to Brains, who had the audacity to take over Hancocks' best-known brew, HB.

Meanwhile, the various big businesses that had swallowed up smaller concerns were themselves swallowed by the Belgian giant Interbrew, which subsequently was forced to sell off parts of its Bass enterprise. These were bought by Coors from across the Atlantic.

Brains celebrated its centenary in 1982 by launching its Century Ale. Two years later the company opened its own shop in St Mary's Street, stocking not only its brewery products but other merchandise as well. This launched the marketing campaign that has proved to be so successful. Brains beer's reputation in the meantime spread ever further. At the London Beer Festival of 1991, Brains Dark won first prize in the mild section. Orders began flooding in from Europe and the United States.

This prompted the company to expand, and it became part of the new marina development in Bath. Back home in Cardiff, a new catering and exporting centre costing £3 million was opened at the old coal site in Bute's East Dock, and Churchill's Hotel was bought for £3 million.

Not every venture prospered. One of its less successful experiments involved trying to enter the lager market, where the big conglomerates ruled. Then, in 1997, Brains bought Crown Buckley. That company had been formed when the family brewery Buckley of Llanelli united with Crown Clubs and created a business that held two hundred pubs and hotels, and had a turnover of £60 million a year.

Brains attracted much criticism for its capture of Crown Buckley. There were protests at the Buckley site in Llanelli and condemnation in the media, but these protests were somewhat appeased when Brains decided to retain one of Buckley's most popular brews, the Reverend James, which was named after James Buckley, the founder of the brewery at Llanelli.

The year of the takeover also marked the closure of Brains' Old Brewery, which was replaced with an entertainment centre where some fifty thousand pints of Brains were pulled for thirsty rugby supporters attending the Rugby World Cup.

Gradually the company has moved ever more widely from Cardiff, buying pubs and hotels as far north as Aberystwyth and from Swansea along the south coast, to Monmouth and beyond the border. In Cardiff, new fashionable café bars were opened, such as Bar Essential, Salt, Bar 88 and the Terra Nova. A chain of catering houses named Highway Taverns was also set up. James Williams, a supply company at Narberth, was swallowed up, as was Steadmans of Newport. Brains went on to buy Innkeepers Wales of Cardigan. The number of company pubs and hotels rose to over two hundred and the brewing total in 2004 was over twenty-five million pints and over eighty thousand barrels.

The company has managed to validate its own slogan 'It's Brains You Want' in more than one way: Brains is no longer Cardiff beer, it is the beer of Wales – and of the world.

Chapter 7

The Canning Town of Wales

Felinfoel Brewery is one of only two big breweries left in Wales. How did it manage to survive while other breweries all around it were closing one by one? One reason for its survival was its success in combining two local products: tin and beer. Felinfoel was the first brewery in Europe – and very nearly the first in the world – to produce and market beer in a can.

The roots of the brewery, which stands on the outskirts of Llanelli, go back to the middle of the 1830s, and industrialist David John's decision to buy the local pub, The King's Head. This was no ordinary hostelry. It was a coaching inn and even had its own smithy where the stagecoach horses were shod.

Because of the political circumstances, the new owner decided to rename the inn. Its royal connection seemed inappropriate considering that Rebecca's horde was active in the area. Their targets were the hated tollgates, and such a tollgate stood across the road from the inn. The inn's name was therefore changed to the Union Inn.

The Union brewed its own beer, initially only during the winter months, and began to supply neighbouring pubs and inns. Then, in 1878, David John decided to build his own brewery across the road on a site where his orchard stood next to his house, Pantglas. The bottling store was sited on the tennis courts. The venture became a success and soon it

David John, founder of Felinfoel Brewery

Felinfoel Brewery today

was employing some fifty workers.

The brewery had a communal function about it. Neighbours who kept pigs in their back gardens would call for the spare mash to feed their animals. When the time came for the animal to be slaughtered, they would take cans of hot water from the brewery to scrape and clean the animal. Water from the brewery was even used for doing the weekly washing. Ladders were borrowed and tools sharpened there.

Ironically, the spot where beer was brewed also had a strong religious connection. During the 1904-05 Revival, many a soul was cleansed by the Reverend Benjamin Humphreys in the waters of the River Lliedi, which ran through the brewery's grounds. There was also a connection with Llanelli's second religion, rugby. It was at the Union Inn that the local rugby club held its weekly meetings. Felinfoel Rugby Club has always been regarded as a preparatory school for playing for Llanelli and Wales. The club's greatest player, no doubt, would be Phil Bennett, who still lives in the village.

The brewery's business began to spread throughout Dyfed's three counties, with the brewery's distinctive sign, the red dragon against a green background, becoming a familiar sight on inn signs. Following David John's retirement, the business passed on to his two sons, David and Martin, his daughter, Mary Anne, and her husband, John Lewis. Unfortunately, Lewis – who was manager of the Wern Iron Works – was a compulsive gambler and a hard drinker. It is said that he lost one tinworks on the turn of a card. In 1920, he shot himself in the brewery office. His widow was made of sterner stuff. Not only did she persevere with the business, but she also ruled with an iron hand. That hand usually carried a heavy cudgel which she was not reluctant to use on any worker who disobeyed her orders. The cudgel can still be seen at the brewery today.

Despite Mary Anne's strict governance, the business hit a bad patch and this was when the idea occurred to the family to combine tin and beer. Their hope was that the two concerns would help each other. Research into the feasibility of producing beer in cans had been ongoing, especially in the United States. Meat, fruit and vegetables were already being canned from as early as 1812, but beer was a different matter. The difficulty was to find a formula that would keep the beer from reacting to the tin. That reaction turned the taste of the contents. There was also the challenge of dealing with the problem of pressure. Felinfoel persevered with the idea, and tinplate sheets from the Metal Box Company at Bynea were sent to London where they were turned into cans.

The revolutionary idea of canning beer made sound sense, as Llanelli was the capital of the tin industry. Indeed, it became known as Tinopolis. On the 3rd of December 1935, the local paper, the *Llanelly and County Guardian* reported on the venture launched at Felinfoel: 'Canned Beer Arrives. Epoch-making Process at Felinfoel Brewery. New Hope for the Tinplate Industry.'

Some of Felinfoel's competitors scorned the idea, and the *Brewers Journal* compared the cans to metal polish tins, such as Brasso containers. The nearby Buckley brewery tried to pour cold water on the whole idea by claiming that they had also developed canned beer but had decided to postpone their launch until the right taste was acquired.

Nevertheless, on the 19th of March 1936 the first batch of Felinfoel's beer in half-pint cans was launched, the first such venture in Europe. The cans were not shaped like those of today, but these had conical tops and clinched caps, exactly like bottle caps.

Felinfoel was only just pipped at the post for the honour of being the first beer cannery in the world. The company that won the race was the Gottfried Krueger Brewery of New Jersey. Even so, Felinfoel claimed a manufacturing victory: before they were able to taste success, Krueger was forced to adapt the beer to suit the cans, while the Llanelli brewery adapted the cans to suit the beer, without destroying the taste.

Within a few months, the contents of some quarter of a million cans had been drunk. By the end of 1936, the brewery had produced a million cans of beer. To celebrate the coronation of George VI in 1936 the brewery produced a special brew, the Famous Strong Ale in cans. It was eventually realised that canning beer was far more expensive than producing bottled beer, and the process was still far from perfect: keeping the beer in the can for too long would lead to the inner wax coating reacting unfavourably with the contents.

The great advantage of canned beer was its easy transportation. Unlike bottles, there was no need to collect the empties. This advantage became evident during the Second World War when Felinfoel secured an exclusive contract to supply NAFFIs, who were in charge of army catering. Despite the German siege, cans of Felinfoel managed to reach the boys at the front: local men stationed on Malta who manned the guns with the Llanelli Territorial Army were able to drink brew produced in their home town, while members of the Desert  rats in North Africa were also able to drink Felinfoel beer.

Exports of cans continued after the war. A Welshman, Terry Beynon of Porth Talbot, who lived in Penang, contracted Felinfoel to send over regular supplies of Double Dragon cans for his Peacock Bar. The brewery began producing special brands for export only, but these were sent in bottles. These included St David's Porter, Prince's Porter, Cream Stout, Heritage Ale and Hercules Strong Ale. During the 1980s, 650 barrels of Felinfoel beer were exported to California.

In the 1950s, however, the business had suffered. After the war, it lost thirty percent of its trade and there was extensive bickering between the John and Lewis families. The company's head office was moved to London, where the Lewises had other businesses, and at all times hovering over the brewery, ready to strike, was Buckleys, situated just a few miles away. It began making offers that Felinfoel found difficult to refuse. Indeed, in 1965 Buckleys made a public offer of £500,000. Although it managed to buy almost half the company's shares and secure a seat on the board, it failed to achieve full control.

Despite these pressures, the management of Felinfoel persevered. The brewery was modernised during the 1970s – a new copper vat was installed – and the head office was moved back home. In 1976 the brewery received a significant boost when its Double Dragon brew won the Challenge Cup as the best barrelled beer at the London Brewers' Exhibition. According to Brian Glover, to the owners and staff this was equal to Wales winning the Rugby World Cup. To add to the celebration, Felinfoel's bitter beer also won a first prize.

Today, Felinfoel has pubs and inns throughout the south west as far north as mid Wales. At the turn of the millennium it could boast pubs in around thirty-five towns and villages. It still excels with its barrelled and smooth beer, including Cambrian Bitter, Double Dragon and Best Bitter. It also produces Felinfoel Stout, and it still produces canned beer. Felinfoel can proudly boast that West is Best.

Chapter 8

Reverential Ale

Buckley's Brewery must be the only commercial brewery in Wales to have been run by a minister of religion, although there is some evidence that a clerk in holy orders, the Reverend G. J. Hughes, was among the subscribers to the Mona Brewery, which was established in Llanfachreth, Ynys Môn in 1841. That brewery is said to have been burnt to the ground by the vengeful widow of the owner of the estate where the brewery had been built. He had died of alcoholism, a victim of the brewery's produce.

Buckleys was a different matter altogether. At Buckleys, the Reverend James Buckley combined the production of ale and communion wine. His name still lives on, thanks to a brew that is named The Reverend James, as a tribute to him.

The story of Buckley's begins in 1760, with the arrival of an eighteen-year-old youth, Henry Child, in Llanelli. He had come from near Haverfordwest to work as an agent for local landlord Sir Thomas Stepney, after whom a street and a hotel in Llanelli's town centre are named. Nine years after he arrived in the town, Child took over The Talbot's Head on lease. Subsequently he did the same with the Carmarthen Arms. Later he built his own inn, The White Lion, and added to his growing business by leasing two corn mills, one at Felinfoel and one at Llanelli. What with his

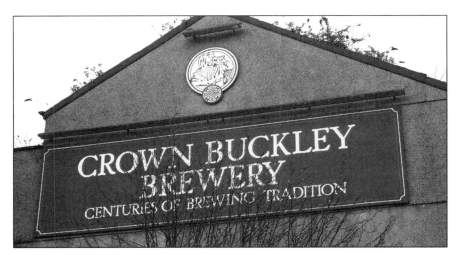

The old Buckley Brewery at Llanelli, now demolished

pubs and grain business, it was little wonder that he then began to brew his own beer. He managed to secure a fifty-five year lease on a piece of land in the Thomas Street area, where he built a brewery.

In 1769, John Wesley visited Llanelli for the first time. This Anglican clergyman and leading theologian of the Methodist movement visited Wales regularly between 1739 and 1790. The man who reputedly travelled two hundred thousand miles and preached forty thousand sermons had a great effect on innkeeper and brewer Henry Child. Indeed, Child experienced a religious conversion, and in 1792 he built a chapel in his own garden in Wind Street, while his house became a haven for itinerant preachers.

One of these visiting preachers was James Buckley, who lived in Oldham. During his trip to Llanelli in 1794 he very nearly lost his life. While crossing the Loughor estuary, he got into difficulties and was assisted by a local man. The event is commorated by a pub at Loughor that is still named The Reverend James.

Following his narrow escape, Buckley was welcomed to stay the night at Child's home, where he met Child's daughter, Maria. They fell in love, and married in 1797. Upon his father-in-law's death, the erstwhile wandering clergyman found himself an established preacher and brewer.

Despite his brewing interests, which later on were mostly tended to by his two sons, Buckley continued with his ministry. It is said that when he was serving at Carmarthen between 1827 and 1929, he discovered that his chapel had been built above a brewery cellar. This discovery inspired a verse by an anonymous poet:

Spirits above and spirits below,
Spirits of bliss, spirits of woe.
The Spirit above is the Spirit Divine,
The spirit below is the spirit of wine.

After his death in 1839, Buckley was buried in the parish churchyard, immediately across the road from his brewery, and the brewing business was continued by his second son, who was also named James. He is described by Brian Glover as 'a Victorian businessman, ruling with a rod of iron for almost as long as Queen Victoria sat sternly on the throne'. He was in charge until his death in 1883 when he was eighty-one years old, having run the business for forty-one years. He was succeeded in turn by his two sons, William and yet another James, and the business changed its name, appropriately, to Buckley Brothers.

Such was the repute of Buckleys that it was visited by the writer and traveller Alfred Barnard in 1890. Following his two-day visit, he described the place as being lofty and most substantially constructed on a four-acre site, with three spacious stores containing nearly seven thousand barrels of ale. Another newly-bought four-storey building was going to stock five thousand barrels. He was very impressed with the brewery's eighteen shire horses, and described the malt house as the largest in Wales.

James Buckley's sudden and untimely death at only fifty-eight years of age in 1859 was a severe blow. He was High Sheriff and a very influential figure who left a personal fortune of £65,000. This left his brother in charge, but William Joseph was soon in trouble as a result of his attempts to buy another brewery, the New Brewery.

The owner of the New Brewery was William Bythway, who had been manager at Buckleys but who had quarrelled with the family over what he regarded as his low wages. He left, and in defiance, he opened his own brewery. Bythway set an asking price of £74,000, which Buckley accepted, but in truth, Bythway had cooked the books and the business was worth less than £20,000. However, Buckley had the last laugh, as the new acquisition substantially added to the brewery's number of pubs, making a total of 216, and a total brewing volume of 36,000 barrels.

Buckleys was made a limited company in 1894. At this time the business was valued at £162,350, and owned or leased 120 public houses. Some 230,000 barrels a year were being sold and the brewery served an area from Tenby to Newcastle Emlyn, Carmarthen, St Clears, Mumbles, Ammanford and Maesteg.

Subsequently, Joseph Buckley decided to buy an additional brewery at Carmarthen – the Carmarthen United Breweries, which was an amalgamation of Norton Brothers and the Merlin Brewery. The unification had caused an uproar and Joseph Buckley took advantage of this to buy the business cheaply in 1900. Three years later, Buckleys won a warrant from the Prince of Wales and a year on won the premier Gold Medal at the London Brewers Exhibition. In 1911, it won a Gold Medal for its beer and stout at the Paris Exhibition. A year earlier, when the Prince of Wales was crowned, Buckleys was appointed Royal Brewers to King George V, the only brewery in Wales to receive such an honour.

The Great War affected Buckleys as it did every brewery in Wales. The company's vehicles were commandeered and sent over to France to transport men and arms and ammunition. As many as sixty-four members of staff were conscripted, and of these, half the number were injured and five were killed. With the war over, the brewery continued as before, and expanded its area from Cardigan Bay to Swansea and the Neath Valley.

The brewery's success attracted potential buyers, but the family refused all offers, stating categorically that the business would never be sold. In the meantime it turned to exporting one of its bottled ales, the Special Welsh Ale, to India and South America and then to South Africa and Australia.

Over the years, the business was unsettled, but it managed to survive the difficulties caused by the Second World War, and it seemed that the company's promise never to sell would hold good. In 1989, the brewery united with the Crown Brewery, but then in 1999 the new company was bought by Brains. Brewing was brought to an end at the Llanelli site, but the family name continued, with Brains continuing to brew a beer called the Reverend James. Today the Buckleys site has been completely cleared as part of a new development scheme in Llanelli town centre.

It seemed that Felinfoel had, at last, seen off its closest neighbour and rival, but the last of the Buckley brewing family at Llanelli would not let the matter drop. Simon Buckley saw the purchase by Brains as a first step towards taking Buckleys out of Wales altogether. He made a hostile bid of £80 million for Brains. His bid was refused. Nevertheless, that was not the end of the story: determined to perpetuate the family brewing tradition, he struck out on his own, and he is still persevering, as detailed in Chapter 13, and is still making waves in the industry. The last of the brewing Buckleys is also a battling Buckley.

Old Buckley pub signs

Chapter 9

The Beer Capital of Wales

Every brewer boasts a personal secret ingredient for his or her success. No brewer, however, would argue against the claim that the nature of the water that is used is of primary importance. It is often the quality of the water that separates good beer from a poor brew, and it was definitely the nature of the water in its vicinity that led to Wrexham being described as 'the Burton of Wales'.

The town has a long and rich tradition of brewing. In Glyndŵr's time, when a blockade prevented food and water from reaching the town, the irate townspeople complained long and loud – not for lack of food and water but for lack of ale.

During the Civil War in the seventeenth century there is evidence that some of Cromwell's men deserted the army in Chester in order to cross the border to drink beer in Wrexham. Later, the quality of Wrexham's beer was blamed for the lateness of the stagecoach leaving the town. The coach would stop in the town for a break, and the travellers loved the local ale so much that they were reluctant to leave.

When itinerant writer George Borrow visited the town during his tour of Wales in 1845, he stopped to converse with a crew of idlers by St Giles' Church. He asked them whether they spoke Welsh:

> 'No, sir,' said the man, 'all the Welsh that any of us know, or indeed wish to know, is Cwrw da.' Here there was a general laugh, Cwrw da signifies good ale … I was subsequently told that all the people of Wrexham are fond of good ale.

Another visitor to the town in 1860 claimed:

> During my stay I have not tasted a mediocre glass! But that which excelled all others was the beverage brewed by Messers. T. Rowlands of the Nag's Head Brewery. We smacked our lips in ecstasy. Two more glasses made us feel quite patriotic and in good humour with everybody, and I shall take pride in extolling the virtues of Wrexham Ale.

At this time, there were nineteen breweries in Wrexham. Twelve of them are listed in *Cwrw Da*, Derek and Beryl Jones' booklet on the inns and ales

The Albion Brewery at Wrexham, the beer capital of Wales

of Wrexham. Such was the town's dependence on brewing that no local cleric would dare condemn alcohol. One brave preacher, Walter Craddock, was frogmarched out of town for condemning the demon drink. However, in 1888 the Reverend David Howell did present in evidence to the House of Lords Select Committee on Sunday Closing the view that Wrexham was more notorious than any other town for its inhabitants' love of strong drink. Another commentator was of the view that the town's ale was a combination of mashed song book pages and boxing gloves, because the local brew would make drinkers want to either sing or fight. According to official records, Wrexham was Britain's most 'fractious' town. In 1849 there were sixty pubs, five ale shops, five shops selling spirits, and twenty licensed shops catering for a population of seven thousand.

The same story persists as late as 1900. An investigation into drinking habits found that throughout Britain there were on average twenty-four public houses for every ten thousand of population. The corresponding figure for Wrexham was forty-six pubs for every ten thousand.

Wrexham was most fortunate in the nature and quality of its water. The Brynffynnon Spring at the lower end of the town was full of beneficial minerals, and the brewing industry grew around it. This was an area of the town where there was no tax imposed on malt, which also proved to be an advantage.

The first Wrexham commercial brewery of any note was established by Edward Thomas in 1799 in an old tannery. It became the Albion Brewery.

Another brewery, the Cambrian in Bridge Street, began brewing in 1844, adopting the Prince of Wales feathers as its emblem. William Sissons, who took over from its manager Joseph Clark, once accused the cities of London and Birmingham of jealously eyeing Welsh water not for drinking but for making beer as good as Wrexham beer.

Another early brewery was the Union, which was established in 1840. The Mitre Brewery at Pentre Felin brewed between 1868 and 1916. Then came the Burton Brewery, bought in 1875 for £541 by Julius Chadwick. He produced a beer described as 'pure Welsh stout', which was regarded as a national drink. Beer brewed at the Sun and Eagle Brewery was sold under the slogan 'Cwrw Da Am Byth', and featured a woman in traditional Welsh dress posing between two barrels.

All these small early breweries were family affairs, established in populated areas where it was difficult to expand, and in the main, they were subsidiary to other businesses. But three substantial businesses did exist: the Soames' Brewery and Island Green Brewery, which would combine to form Border Breweries, and Peter Walker's brewery.

Walker was a brewing legend. The original Walker began brewing in Ayr in Scotland before moving south to Liverpool, where he and his son established a brewing empire (the name of Walker still survives in a chain of pubs owned by the Carlsberg-Tetley concern in Liverpool).

Peter Walker, very much aware of being overshadowed by his brother Andrew, who built a brewing empire from Birkenhead to Newcastle and as far afield as Belfast and Dublin, moved to Wales in the late 1830s where he was apprenticed to Joseph Clark at the Cambrian Brewery. He then began in business by buying the small Willow Brewery and went on to transform it into Wrexham's largest brewery business. His stature in the community grew, and he was twice made Mayor. He bought a new pulpit for the Parish Church, bought a ceremonial mace for the Town Corporation, and rebuilt the bridge close to his brewery at his own expense. He was on course for his third term as Mayor, but when another brewer, Thomas Rowlands of the Nag's Head, was chosen ahead of him, he took offence. He stayed on as a resident of the town, living at Coed y Glyn close to Erddig Park, but he moved his business to Burton on Trent and soon afterwards the Willow Brewery was abandoned.

At Burton, Walker designed a huge brewery, but like Moses before him, he only got to glimpse the promised land. Before he could claim it, he died, soon after he had laid the foundation stone. His funeral was the largest ever seen in Wrexham.

The Walker brewing story does not quite end there, however. In 1890, the family name returned to the town when the Warrington brewery, set up by Peter Walker's brother Andrew, bought the Union Brewery in Wrexham. But in 1927, the company sold its twenty-seven pubs, and Island Green bought around half of them. The demise of the Union Brewery also left the market open for Island Green to go on and buy Soames' Brewery, previously the Nag's Head, the only serious competitor left by 1933.

The Nag's Head already had a good reputation and in 1870 it had been bought by Henry Aspinall, who in four years formed Wrexham Breweries. His beer won a Gold Medal at the Albert Hall Exhibition in London in 1875. Despite this success, the company went to the wall with debts of £50,000. It was bought by Arthur Soames of Nottinghamshire, and he set up his son, Frederick, as manager of the newly named Soames' Brewery. During the next decade the business tripled in size. When that well-known visitor Alfred Barnard came to Wrexham in 1892, Soames' Brewery was the only brewery deemed important enough to visit. He praised the business, especially the production of 'true Welsh ale' and also a beverage named Guinea Wrexham, which he described as 'a household and family ale'.

Like Peter Walker before him, Frederick Soames of the Soames' Brewery was elected Mayor, in 1921 and in 1922, when Queen Victoria visited the town. Indeed, Soames went one better than Walker and was made Mayor three times. His pub empire spread up as far as the northern tip of Ynys Môn and he named his business The Welsh Ale Brewery. By the time of his death in 1926 he had created a business that owned over one hundred pubs.

At the onset of the Great War, one of Soames' wagons was sent to the front with the brewery's name still emblazoned on its sides. In fact, the vehicle was shelled but this attracted considerable publicity for the brewery.

In 1922 there were eight breweries still in business in Wrexham, but after Soames' death in 1926, brewing in the town dwindled. Nevertheless, Soames' Brewery survived and became a limited company in 1931, retaining a member of the family at the helm. After only two months, however, it was successfully taken over by Island Green.

Soames' Brewery and Island Green, which had been founded in 1856 on Caea farm by William and John Jones, had been old adversaries. The two businesses stood only a quarter of a mile apart. On the 27th of June 1931 they were united, together with Dorsett Owen of Oswestry, to create Border Brewery. This was an appropriate name as it operated on both sides of the border. Soon, the Island Green site was closed. In 1938, however, Border went public and the red dragon was adopted as its

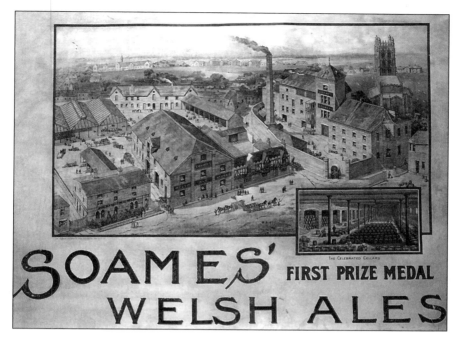

A poster advertising Soames' beer.

emblem. During the war, the Luftwaffe created a one-off smoky brew: a German bomb landed on Rhos Mountain and the thick smoke from the fire it caused hung over the town for a week, and the smoke infiltrated the beer. Rather than waste it, the brew was re-mixed and sold with no one any the wiser.

By 1960, Border owned over two hundred pubs, but its future did not look bright and the brewery's morale was low. Whitbread, which had already joined the Flowers brewery, bought a considerable amount of the company's shares. It was intent on buying Border but had little interest in the site. Border continued to struggle on into the 1970s and, indeed, celebrated its silver jubilee in 1983. It still owned a valuable asset – the Racecourse Ground, Wrexham Football Club's home ground, with its adjacent Turf Tavern.

The end, though not unexpected, came in an unexpected way. Border was bought by Marstons of Burton rather than Whitbread, although it was done with Whitbread's consent. After all, Whitbread held a significant number of shares in both companies. Then, in 1986, where Hitler had failed, vandals succeeded. Border Brewery went up in flames,

Chapter 10

The Lager Legacy

If a prize was awarded for Wales' most internationally successful alcoholic drink, then Wrexham Lager would be a leading contender. At the height of its popularity, it exported its product worldwide. There is evidence that it was supped in General Gordon's palace in Khartoum in 1898. During the Second World War, a mid-Atlantic pact between Roosevelt and Churchill was sealed with a toast of Wrexham Lager. The drink was also sold on ocean-going liners such as The Mauritania and The Queen Elizabeth.

Real ale aficionados tend to scorn lager. It is said that the difference between lager and real ale is that the former is passed through at least seven pairs of kidneys before it is bottled or casked. Be that as it may, lager sales over the past forty years have claimed half the brewing market in Britain. But it was a very late arrival. Although in 1913 lager sold very little in Britain, ninety percent of the world's beer was lager. When it did arrive, Wrexham stood shoulder to shoulder with London in the campaign for its recognition. For over a century, Wrexham and lager were bracketed together as naturally as Penclawdd and cockles, or Caerffili and cheese.

The story of Wrexham Lager begins in Manchester, where a gathering of wealthy immigrants from Germany and Czechoslovakia were intent on displacing the warm lager of their adopted country with the cold and clear lager of the lands of their birth. As Wrexham already had a good brewing reputation, it was there, on the 6th of May 1881, that the Wrexham Lager Beer Company was formed. Among the founding members were chemists, bankers and textile merchants.

Penadur Springs were originally earmarked for brewing purposes, but unfortunately the water lacked the necessary quality, and another well was chosen to the west of the town. This possessed the qualities for producing a Pilsner type of lager, not unlike that brewed in Czechoslovakia. Barley was no problem as it was grown extensively around nearby Shrewsbury. The brewery was built close to the two railway stations, but this was no ordinary brewery: it cost £20,000 to build, and another £10,000 was spent on the brewing plant, which included freezing equipment capable of producing five thousand tons of ice annually. *The Wrexham Advertiser* reported:

About 40 years ago lager beer brewing was cultivated only in one German province. Since that period, however, the whole of Germany,

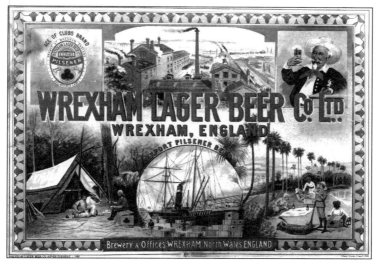

A Wrexham Lager sign noting that the town was in England

Austria, Scandinavia, Holland, Belgium, France, Russia, America and even Japan have adopted lager beer brewing. The greatest obstacle for England [sic] was the difficulty in procuring cheap ice. This difficulty is now put aside by the excellent ice machines manufactured today.

The Advertiser had rather jumped the gun. Brewing began in 1883 but things went wrong from the very beginning. The ice machines were in fact incapable of delivering sufficient ice. In countries where natural ice was plentiful, there was no problem, but creating ice artificially was another matter and it meant that at Wrexham, the only type of lager it was possible to produce was a dark Bavarian type rather than the Pilsner they had envisaged.

Some have asserted that the Wrexham lager brewery provided the first lager brewed in the United Kingdom, but according to Brian Glover this is not the case. It was indeed the first lager brewery to be established as a company, but the first drops of lager to be produced in the UK were brewed in a London brewery, the Austro-Bavarian and Crystal Ice Factory in Tottenham, which produced Bavarian lager at the end of 1882.

Gradually, sales of Wrexham Lager picked up, but not by nearly enough. It was sold at the Royal Jubilee Exhibition of 1887 and even during the Wrexham National Eisteddfod the following year, but it is doubtful that the winning Chair and Crown poets, Tudno and Elfed respectively – two ministers of religion – celebrated by drinking Wrexham

Lager. Elfed's winning ode, incidentally, was entitled 'Sunday in Wales'. His Sunday would have been a dry Sunday.

Soon after, the lager companies in both Wrexham and London went bust. At Wrexham a chemist called Robert Graesser, who was also Director of the Monsanto Chemical Company, came to the rescue. Following a chance meeting with one of the brewery directors, Ivan Levenstein, he bought off the Wrexham Lager Beer Company's assets and debts as a majority shareholder. He immediately installed mechanical refrigeration equipment. He also installed brine coils and managed to lower the cellar temperature considerably. This led to the production of a light lager and a Pilsner-style lager as well as the original dark. Unfortunately, sales remained low.

This posed a new problem – that of how to persuade traditional beer drinkers to adapt to lager drinking. The company decided to promote Wrexham Pilsner Lager in a reverse advertising campaign. Rather than boasting its strength, they maintained that it was comparatively weak, but that its strength lay in its weakness. In short, Wrexham Lager was presented first and foremost as a tonic rather than as an alcoholic drink. Its Certificate of Purity stated:

> The Wrexham Lager Beer Company has been successful in producing a light Pilsner Lager Beer which not only refreshes, but acts as a tonic in cases of weak digestion and is almost non-intoxicating. When more generally known and consumed, it will diminish intoxication and do more for the temperance cause than all the efforts of the total abstainers.

What magnificent spin! In truth, it was only one-and-a-half percent weaker than ordinary beer.

Again, sales did not reach the necessary level, especially in the Wrexham area. Nevertheless, Graesser persevered. He began selling his company's brew in the towns and cities of England. In fact, it was easier to buy Wrexham Lager at London watering holes such as the Carlton Club and the Constitutional Club than it was in Wrexham pubs. Graesser even secured a contract to sell Wrexham Lager to the British Army. Then came his master stroke. In 1904, he crossed to the United States on the SS Baltic, taking with him a quantity of his lager. Despite the distance and the time spent on board, the lager retained its composition, something other companies had failed to achieve. This opened the door to the sale of Wrexham Lager on board liners and to foreign markets. By the beginning of the twentieth century, the brewery was almost wholly dependent on foreign sales. Wrexham Lager was exported from Wales to the Caribbean, the South Sea Islands, Brazil, Australia, New Zealand, Africa and the United States.

On the 5th of October 1898, a letter was received by the brewery from a staff sergeant from his post in the Sudan. Enclosed with the letter were labels from a Wrexham Lager Beer bottle that had been found in the grounds of General Gordon's palace in Khartoum. When Kitchener relieved Khartoum, it is said that a stock of Wrexham Lager was found in Gordon's palace.

When Graesser died in 1911, he was succeeded by his five sons and one daughter. One of the sons, Edgar, ran the brewery. By now the local miners had accepted the lager brewed amongst them, especially the dark type. During the Great War, despite suspicions about its foreign connections, the company managed to survive, but its head brewer and the brewery's engineer, both Germans, were interned on the Isle of Man. The company also had enemies inside the trade. Local brewers, intent on promoting their own product, united successfully in persuading pubs to boycott Wrexham Lager. The company responded by expanding its sales in English towns and cities, and in 1922 the company struck back locally by buying its first Wrexham pub, The Cross Foxes, which stood adjacent to the brewery. It was there that lager, genuinely chilled, was first sold in Britain. The pub sold over thirty barrels of lager a week dispensed through ice boxes.

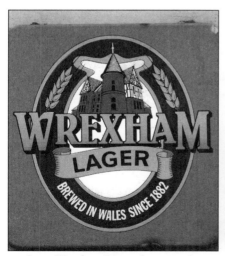

Some Wrexham Lager signs remain, though production has run dry.

The red brick brewery tower that used to be a Wrexham landmark.

Meanwhile, exports continued. During one Christmas in the 1930s, three train-loads of casks left Wrexham for world cruise ships departing London and Southampton. The lager could now keep its perfect condition for at least twelve months. The lager was also part of an historic occasion: when Churchill and Roosevelt signed a war-time agreement between Britain and the USA in the mid-Atlantic, they sealed it by touching glasses filled with Wrexham Lager. This lease-lend agreement marked the end of America's isolationism.

The company proved its marketing prowess by offering to outlets exactly what they craved. The famous Ace of Clubs logo was aimed at the American market. For the Irish Republic market, where anti-British sentiment was strong, it was noted on the labels that the brewery's Club Lager was bottled in Ireland. In the meantime the passenger liner sales grew apace when a contract was signed with Cunard. Closer to home, a contract was signed between Wrexham Lager and the Great Western Railway, an agreement that opened the door to selling lager on trains and in the company's hotels and restaurants.

Locally, the company strengthened its hold by buying twenty-three Beirnes pubs. By the time of the Second World War, the company was selling over eighty-five percent of its products to the armed forces. On the negative side, the company suffered significant war losses: merchant ships carrying its lager were torpedoed and its bottling centre at Liverpool was bombed. The allied victory was celebrated with a special brew named Victory.

In 1949 the company was taken over by Ind Coope and Allsopp. The merged companies subsequently bought a Scottish brewery, and the brewing business moved there, leaving Wrexham idle. Locals were further incensed when the name Wrexham Lager was replaced by Graham Lager. In 1963, however, a brand new brewery was built in the

The Horse and Jockey, one of Wrexham's most famous watering holes

town, one of the most up-to-date breweries in Europe, employing 240 staff and with a brewing capacity of eighteen thousand barrels.

When Ind Coope, the parent company, became part of Allied Breweries, forming one of the biggest concerns in Britain, it immediately invested an extra £4 million in Wrexham. But increasingly the company turned towards the Continental market.

In 1978 the name Wrexham Lager was revived, and the company celebrated its centenary in 1982 with a re-launch of its dark and its Pilsner lager, as well as, temporarily, the Ace of Clubs label, which had been sold. In 1990, Wrexham Lager won the International Brewing Industry's Championship Trophy at Burton on Trent. Allied then merged with Carlsberg's British branch, Carlsberg-Tetley. The new brewing giant decided to concentrate on its Scholls line, and ignored Wrexham Lager. It continued to be produced in Leeds, but only in name: soon it was abandoned to its fate, as the company neglected its peculiar qualities and the great care it deserved in its manufacture. In 2001, some 110 workers lost their jobs in Wrexham. The most modern brewery in Europe now found that it had no room to expand.

Wrexham Lager still refuses to go quietly. Clwyd South-East MP Martyn Jones, himself an ex-member of the Wrexham Lager staff, has a mission to revive the product. Mr Jones, who worked as a microbiologist between 1969 and 1987, including over two years' experience in Burton, has an agreement with Carlsberg-Tetley. He was promised the right to buy the Wrexham Lager brand for one pound when its production ceased completely. He now owns the name of the Wrexham Lager Beer Company and awaits the day when Wrexham Lager is again brewed in the town. He is prepared to hand over both the brand name and the company name to whoever will brew a lager of quality once more in Wrexham.

At the time of going to press, Mr Jones revealed that he had a financial backer who also owns a chain of outlets. Should anything go wrong, he has a back-up plan involving a brewer of bitter who could also brew lager. Thwaites of Leeds have offered cooperation in expertise and advertising, and the Wrexham Economic Development Committee is interested in finding a suitable site.

In the meantime, a group of Wrexham Football Club supporters has formed a Trust in an effort to save the club and to revive Wrexham Lager. The Trust has cooperated with local brewer Pene Coles of the Jolly Brewer in launching two beers. One is a Stella Artois-type of lager named Benno, as a tribute to ex-Wrexham star Gary Bennett. The other, a dark lager, will be named Tommy, after another star, Tommy Bamford. As far as Wrexham Lager is concerned, the dream lives on.

Chapter 11

The Golden Apples of the Tun

The nearest thing we have to a national drink is probably cider. The residents of Breconshire, Radnorshire and Monmouthshire would certainly agree. J. Geraint Jenkins observes that the drinking of cider on Breconshire farms in the 1930s was so widespread that a certain Calvinistic Minister who was attending a preaching session at Trefeca described the shire in 1934 as 'a cider besotten county'.

It is little wonder that the fermented juice of the apple was despised so much by the fire and brimstone brigade. After all, even though the Book of Genesis does not specify the genus of the Tree of Good and Evil in the Garden of Eden, it is widely regarded as having been an apple tree.

It is known that apple trees grew along the Nile Delta as early as 1300 BC although it is unclear when cider was first produced. By 55 BC, however, the Romans arriving in Britain discovered that villagers on the east coast were drinking a cider-like tipple and even Julius Caesar himself was much taken by it.

By the beginning of the ninth century, cider drinking was well established in Europe, as Charlemagne testifies. After the Norman conquest, orchards were planted in Britain specifically for the propagation of cider apples. In the Middle Ages, cider-making was a proper industry, with monasteries selling strong and spicy cider to pilgrims and locals alike, especially on the continent. Cider allowances were paid to farm workers, and by the mid-seventeenth century almost every farm in the apple-growing areas had its own cider press.

Changes in the pattern of agriculture resulted in a slump in cider-making. Gradually, during the twentieth century, a revival was seen and cider began to be mass-produced, but it is only recently that traditional cider-making has been revived.

Emigrants from Britain to the USA took with them seeds for growing cider-apple trees, and during the colonial period, cider became so popular that a town's prosperity was judged by the volume of cider it produced. Despite the slump in the drinking of alcohol generally during Prohibition, cider-making now is back in business in the USA.

The Celts seem to have taken to cider in a big way. In Brittany, especially, cider-making has always been – and remains – a traditional industry. *Cidre Bouché* is a very popular drink there. As J. Geraint Jenkins notes, cider-making was practised on many farms in Wales until recent

Two cider presses: Lodge Farm, Raglan c. 1955, and Brecon Fair, 1957.

times, and cider orchards that grew such varieties as Golden Pippin, Redstreak, Kingston Black, Old Foxwhelp, Perthyre and Trederick were well distributed throughout the border counties. Many pubs also had cider houses with their own milling and pressing plants, and in the border counties, cider seems to have been the most popular drink amongst the countrymen.

Jenkins describes the method of making cider in Brecknockshire in some detail:

> Harvesting of apples was carried out in October and November, but the fruit was not picked; the trees were shaken so that the ripe apples fell to the ground. They were then piled into heaps in the orchard to mature for a week or two.
>
> The apples were then carted to the cider house, usually a brick or stone building, but occasionally an open-sided thatched shed. This contained a horse-driven stone cider mill for crushing the apples into pomace, or 'must', and a press for pressing the pomace to extract the juice.

Such a cider press can be seen at the National History Museum at St Fagans. It was taken from Llanginon and preserved for posterity. It is made of Forest of Dean Millstone Grit and is seven feet in diameter. Constructed of three separate parts clamped together, it runs in a chase that is eighteen inches wide and hollowed out to a depth of nine inches. The rim has a massive runner stone, weighing nearly two tons and measuring three to four feet in diameter.

The mill was worked by means of a wooden framework carrying shafts to which a horse or donkey was harnessed. The frame was then pushed rather than pulled, in a clockwise direction.

Prior to the appearance of the cider mill during the seventeenth century, apples were pulped in large mortars with long-handled pestles. It took three or four men a whole day to manage twenty to thirty bushels. In Brecknockshire, this method was used up to the middle of the nineteenth century.

Another method used in the area was the breaker, which was a mangle with toothed rollers. Originally this was turned by a horse, and later by a donkey engine. Itinerant cider makers used such methods until very recently at the New Inn at Talgarth, which is reputedly the last Welsh public house where cider was made.

Whatever method was used, the crushed pomace would be transferred with wooden shovels into wooden buckets and then to the press, a huge wooden apparatus which had at its base a heavy stone slab. The most common form was the pack press, in which a sheet of hessian or sisal – in Brecknockshire, horse-hair mats were widely used – was placed across the bottom of the square frame above the trough. A thick layer of pomace was spread over the mat, which was then folded over the pomace. This was repeated until layers of matting and pomace filled the frame. The press was then racked down onto the layers, forcing out the juice into the trough.

The freshly-produced juice could be fermented immediately, but sometimes it would be stored for future conversion into cider. Yeasts are naturally present in apple skins, so the first kind of fermentation occurs naturally. A second form of fermentation involves lactic acid bacteria, which is also present in apple juice. The fermented juice would usually be left to mature for five or six months.

Casks filled with cider, awaiting maturity, would be sealed with mixtures of clay, cow dung, chaff and ashes. Sometimes pieces of fresh meat would be placed in the casks to add to the flavour. Seven to ten hundredweights of apples would be needed to produce fifty-two gallons, or a hogshead of cider. The remaining pomace would be used as pig swill.

Jenkins notes that the art of cider making has all but disappeared from the traditional Welsh areas. He attributes this to 'the constant preaching of temperance by Nonconformist ministers, the depletion of the farm labour force and the disappearance of draught horses for driving mills'. Lately, however, Wales has witnessed a revival, and the Welsh Perry and Cider Association in Wales currently lists twenty-three producers.

In mid Wales, there are now numerous cider producers. Ralph's Cider and Perry is based in New Radnor, and Ralph, who was encouraged by memories of his father, has been producing since 1976 and was at one time farm manager for Bertram Bulmer of Bulmers Cider. The 1982 vintage was deemed by Bulmers themselves to be the best-tasting cider analysed by the company that year.

At Builth Wells, D. Wynn Brown makes Piston Broke Club Cider from chosen varieties of apples hand-picked in ancient organic orchards. They are pressed in a vintage French press powered by a Massey Ferguson tractor. The cider is then matured in oak barrels that once held rum. There are no additives or preservatives.

In 2001, Seidir O Sir/Welsh Country Cider was founded at Betws Diserth in 2001 by Trevor Powell. The first two hundred gallons were donated back to the earth. Apple types used are Kingston Black, Vilberie, Strawberry Norman, Michelin, Yarlington Mill and a few Harry Master's Jersey from the company's own embryonic orchard. The production in

2001/2 was five hundred gallons. Others producing in mid Wales are Edw – Mervyn Davies of Aberedw near Builth Wells – and Montgomery Cidermakers of Garthmyl.

In west Wales, Tojola Cider of Dihewyd near Lampeter make cider and perry, and owners Kevin and Nikki Sweet have also planted a hundred-tree show orchard using only Welsh varieties of apple and pear trees. They hope to run residential courses on rural activities, including the making of cider. The ciders they produce are Drunk Dewi, an oak cask cider; Guinivere, which is dark gold and clear; Gallahad, which is sweet and oaky; Igrayne, cloudy gold and sweet; Lancelot, which has a fruity medium flavour; Merlin's Mist, which is deep gold, cloudy and dry; Pendragon, gold and clear, and Queen Mab, with a deep and dry flavour. Alcohol content varies from 5.8 to 7.5 percent.

Another west Wales maker is Gethin ap Dafydd, who runs Sudd Cwmpo Drosto (Falling-over Juice) at Haverfordwest. He began four years ago and used local apples gathered from hedges around his home. He now buys in apples from Monmouthshire and produces three hundred gallons a year. He sells his product through an agent, supplying two pubs in Pembrokeshire. He hopes to invest in setting up his own orchard.

In St Dogmael's near Cardigan, Richard Cooper produces cider at the Abbey Apple Co-operative.

Five cider producers are listed for Glamorgan. One of these, Gwynt y Ddraig, produced by the Welsh Cider and Perry Company at Llanilltyd Faerdre, has broken through and is stocked by Wetherspoons and Brains. Andy Gronow and Bill George first made cider in the autumn of 2001 and now they produce a range of ten ciders and two perries. In 2003/4, the company produced fourteen hundred gallons. The ciders are Orchard Gold; Fiery Fox; Major Brown; Gold Medal – Medium (winner of CAMRA's Gold Medal in 2004); Black Dragon, made from Kingston Black; Haymaker – Medium, which is bittersweet and sharp; Barking Mad, a strong medium dry; Stoke Red, which is dry and oak fermented; Drew's Brew – Medium Sweet, and Bill's Bootleg. The perries are Two Trees and Starlight.

Seidr Dai is produced by Dai and Fiona Matthews in Cyncoed, Cardiff. Production began in 2002 and the ciders are all made from Welsh fruit, and the apples hand-picked. Wherever possible, rarer varieties are used. Dave founded the Welsh Cider Society in 2001. Ciders are all available on draught and include Thorn, which is a perry; Berllanderi Blend 2003, from the orchard of the same name; Gwehelog; Panker's Pride, a blend of pears; Crwys Fach, made from locally-grown pears; Major Tom and Major

An orchard in bloom at y Fenni and, right, apples being pressed by hand and, below, by steam press in Radnorshire

Tom II; Dai's Dry, and Blakeny Red, Rock, and Burgundy, all of which are perries. Annual production in 2003/4 was 750 gallons. This year, the Mathews' perry won the CAMRA Gold Award.

Seidr Alarch, or Swan Cider, is made by Dave Jones at Llantrisant. He began producing from hand-picked apples in 2004. The apples are also hand-sorted, hand-washed and hand-pressed. Annual production in 2005/6 was 445 litres, and ciders include Black Swan; Cygnet '05; Swanderful, and McPhee 9.5, which is only for personal consumption. Two perries are also produced.

Others producing in Glamorgan include Bragdy Brodyr, run by Richard Williams at Glynneath, and Mill Cider at the Gower Heritage Centre.

By far the largest concentration of cider makers is found in Gwent, where around a dozen producers are listed. Seidr Mynediad Ysbyty (Hospital Admission Cider) is made by Jon Hallam at Monmouth. He began in 1982 with his Seidr Hen Ffordd Gymreig o Fyw (The Old Welsh Way of Life), a Tom Putt single variant. He prides himself on the fact that his great uncle made cider near Leominster over sixty years ago. Indeed, he maintains that it was one of his forebears who invented the term 'to scrump'.

Annual production in 2001/2 was two hundred gallons and he lists among his products Ellis' Bitter/Red Vallis; Ellis' Blend, his main commercial cider, and Deity Grade, which uses Monmouthshire forest fruit, and water from local holy wells.

Springfield Cider is made by Alan and Jo Wordsworth at Llangofan, between Raglan and Monmouth. The sixty-acre bush orchards and eighteen thousand trees at Springfield Farm were planted in 1998. The Wordsworth's first harvest in 2003 was a huge success. The company's products include Farmhouse, a bittersweet; Old Bar, which is strong and fruity; Faraway, and Sledgehammer, which has an alcohol content of 8.4 percent.

Troggi Seidr is produced at Earlswood by Dr Mike Penney. It was founded in 1984 using milling and pressing equipment based at Usk College. The company installed its own equipment in 1995. Specialising in whole juice dry cider and perry, its products include Troggi Seidr and Troggi Seidr Perry. Production in 2001/2 was 3,500 litres.

Other Gwent producers include Blaengawney Cider, Newbridge; CJ's Cider, Penrhos, Raglan; Clytha Perry at the Clytha Arms near Abergavenny; Cobourn Cider, Grosmont; Three Saints at Llantrisant, Usk; Usk Cider, Wernddu Vinyard, Pen y Clawdd and W. M. Watkin & Sons, Grosmont.

Only one cider maker is listed in north Wales: Steve Hughes of Llandegla who makes Rosie's Triple D. In 2006 it was awarded the CAMRA 2006 award for the best bottled cider.

For those interested in cider or perry production it is worth noting that the Dolau Hirion Nursery at Llandeilo specialises in supplying rare and unusual trees.

Chapter 12

Welsh Whisky

The honour of producing Wales' first whisky distillation is attributed to the monks of Ynys Enlli (Bardsey Island) in around 356 AD. Rheuallt Hir is reputed to have adapted a distilling process brought to Wales by early Greek merchants. He used their methods to distil the sweet ale or braggot produced by the Enlli monks and then added honey and herbs.

We have to wait until 1705 for the next reputed Welsh distillery, which was founded at Dale, Pembrokeshire by the Williams family. Evan Williams, a descendant, emigrated to America, moving firstly to Virginia and then to Kentucky in 1780, where he settled. He grew crops, but because of the difficulty in transporting his grain to market, he decided to produce whisky, setting up his distillery on the banks of the Ohio on what is now Fifth Street, Louisville. He was made a Member of the Board of Trustees of Louisville but he angered the city fathers by insisting on bringing one of his bottles of whisky with him to every meeting. Although censured, he never left with a full bottle. He was appointed Harbour Master and oversaw the building of the city jail between 1802 and 1803. He is considered to be Kentucky's first distiller. Evan Williams whisky and bourbon is still produced at the Heaven Hill Breweries in Louisville.

Another American distiller, Jack Daniel, is also reputed to have been a Welshman from the Cardigan area, but there is no proof that he was in fact Welsh. In *The Jack Daniel Legacy*, Ben A. Green claims that Joseph Daniel moved from England to Scotland, where he married and from where he emigrated to America. His grandson Jasper 'Jack' Newton Daniel founded the whisky empire – not bourbon – at Lynchburg, Tennessee, having learned his trade from Dan Call, a Lutheran minister.

The first Welsh distillery of note – and the only one until recently – was that set up near Bala in 1889 when the Welsh Whisky Company was registered with a capital of £100,000. The man behind the venture was the squire of the Rhiwlas Estate, R. J. Lloyd Price, an entrepreneur, huntsman and eccentric. Price founded an industry on the banks of the Tryweryn river at Fron-goch, where he set up a brush factory, slate quarries, a table water plant, a slaughterhouse, brickworks and clay pits, and sold various minerals including Fuller's Earth. There are houses still standing at Fron-goch which were built entirely from locally-made products. The industrious squire also turned the Rhiwlas Estate into the largest game farm in Britain.

The distillery was his most ambitious scheme, an idea that was sparked while Price was attending sheep-dog trials at Hyde Park in London in 1887, an activity that he himself originated. In fact, the first ever sheep-dog trials were held near Bala in 1873. While attending the Hyde Park event he chanced to mention whisky to his friend Robert Willis, who challenged him to emulate the Scots and the Irish by producing native whisky. Two years later, Welsh whisky was flowing at Fron-goch.

The advertising blurb was composed by Lloyd Price himself and is a masterpiece of hype. Published in his pamphlet, *The Truth*, it describes Fron-goch whisky as:

> ... the most wonderful whisky that ever drove the skeleton from the feast, or painted landscapes in the brain of man. It is the mingled souls of peat and barley, washed white within the rivers of the Tryweryn. In it you will find the sunshine and shadow that chased each other over the billowy fields, the breath of June, the carol of the lark, the dew of night, the wealth of summer, the autumn's rich content, all golden and imprisoned light. Drink it and you will hear the voice of men and maidens singing the 'Harvest Home' mingled with the laughter of children. Drink it, and you will feel within your blood the startled dawns, the dreamy tawny husks of perfect days. Drink it, and within your soul will burn the bardic fire of the Cymri, and their law-abiding earnestness. For many years this liquid joy has been within staves of oak, longing to touch the lips of man, nor will its prototype from the Sherry Casks distain the more dulcet labial entanglement with any New or Old Woman.

In *The Truth* he also included the following verse with an illustration of a dancing 'John Jones' presenting a bottle of whisky to 'Jenny':

> Why, with capers so many
> John Jones, gay you are?
> Welsh whisky, dear Jenny
> From Bala, "bur ddha".

In August 1889, Queen Victoria visited the Bala area and Lloyd Price presented her with a cask of Welsh whisky. This gave him the opportunity to add the words 'By Royal Appointment' to his whisky adverts. Another cask was presented to the Prince of Wales in 1894 by the Bala Freemasons'

Concentration Camp. Frongoch. Bala.

The old Fron-goch distillery, where German and Irish prisoners were kept, and how it appears today

The Penderyn distillery today

Lodge, of which Lloyd Price was a member.

Lloyd Price's dream was to produce a whole range of whiskies bearing labels such as Black Prince, Men of Harlech, Maid of Llangollen, Saint David, Taffy, Welsh Rare Bit, Bells of Aberdovey and The Leek. Unfortunately, the whisky venture lasted only ten years. Although the Welsh temperance movement has been blamed for its demise, it seems more than likely that it was the product's lack of quality that was to blame. In 1966, H. A. Lloyd states in *Country Quest* that while the whisky, in cask, was fine, it was a different matter in bottle. Bottled, the whisky remained crude and rough and seemed to 'mature backwards'. It was described in Harper's as 'eating its own head'.

The company was finally dissolved on the 3rd of January 1899, some four years before the great Methodist revival that has been blamed by some errant historians for the venture's demise. Fron-goch whisky today is a rare commodity. The last time a bottle went on auction in September 2001 it reached £1,350. There are at least a dozen bottles still in existence.

During the 1970s, an attempt to revive Welsh malt whisky was made by Dafydd Gittins with his Swn y Môr (Sound of the Sea). He and Mal Morgan began blending whisky in a small cellar at Brecon in 1974. Later the venture moved to a brewhouse behind the Camden Arms Hotel, where Gittins and his wife Gillian formed the Brecon Brewery. The whisky itself seemed to be a Scottish blend with added herbs. Even so, it was popular, especially when sold in rugby-ball shaped bottles. They followed Swn y Môr with the single malt Prince of Wales.

In 1990, the couple formed the Welsh Whisky Company Ltd and a year later production moved to the Ffrwdgrech Estate. New products were introduced, including Merlyn Cream Liqueur, Tafski Vodka and Glan Usk Gin. In 1995, the company, which had relied on foreign distillates, announced that it would begin home-distilled production at its new £70,000 distillery. Their intent was to produce three 3,000-litre batches a week, the equivalent of five hundred bottles, with production likely to treble within two years. Deals were made with supermarkets Tesco, Asda and Makro, but alas, it was not to be. Pressure from jealous Scottish distillers led to litigation and allegations of duty fraud. So another five years had to pass before whisky was distilled on Welsh soil for the first time in over a hundred years.

Penderyn Single Malt Whisky began life, appropriately, on Saint David's Day. What was described by the company as 'The Gold Rush' started on the 1st of March 2004 when a limited number of first-release bottles was made available. The following year, the Penderyn distillery opened its visitors' centre and added to its products the Brecon Special

Reserve Dry Gin, Brecon Premium Vodka and Merlyn, the cream liqueur.

Penderyn is named after the village in the Brecon Beacons where it is based, a place with connections with Dic Penderyn, who was wrongfully executed in 1831 for his part in the Merthyr Riots. The whisky is produced in a purpose-built distillery using the latest in modern technology. One of the brains behind the venture is Dr Faraday of the University of Surrey, a descendant of the famous physicist Sir Michael Faraday. Dr Faraday designed the distilling process. Recognised whisky authority Dr Jim Swann is also involved. He remarks that Penderyn has 'a smooth, unique style, delicate and full of flavour and is dangerously easy to drink'.

The single malt that was produced first was allowed to mature in oak casks once used by the Evan Williams and Jack Daniel's distilleries. It was then finished in Madeira barrels to deliver what is described by the company as a distinctive, golden, single malt that is light on the palate and smooth to taste.

The Company's produce not only tastes good, it is also packaged tastefully and attractively. They have sounded out the possibility of exports, especially to America. It has signed a two-year deal with the Welsh Rugby Union and there are plans to create a special product to mark the Ryder Cup Golf competition visiting Wales in 2010 at the Celtic Manor.

Chapter 13

The Fox Returns

Although the Buckley's brewing dynasty came to an end with the Brains take-over, the family name lives on, thanks to a sixth generation descendant who brews in Llandeilo under the company name William Evan Evans. Simon Buckley's desk is overhung by the last Buckley flag to flutter over the old Llanelli site, which has now been flattened by developers.

In 1967, at the behest of his cousin, Kemmis Buckley, Simon gave up his dream of studying to be a chartered surveyor at Reading University, to work on the shop floor at the family brewery. There he rose from being a junior brewer to learning every aspect of the trade – bottling, kegging and aspects of production. During his nine years there he learnt to appreciate quality and adopted what he calls a brand vision. Dominating his thoughts was Buckley's 220 years of heritage and the great sense of pride in working in what was, in effect, a village within a town. As he remarked to me when we met:

> I was seen as the security for the future. It confirmed my belief that family brewing in Wales was something that should be preserved and cherished and not something that should be gifted away. Unfortunately, some saw me, a live wire, strong-willed and someone who was relatively bright, as a threat. I probably joined five years too soon. The workforce, however, made me feel welcomed. And I hang the brewery flag above my desk to remind myself that never again will the Buckley brewing business be forsaken to outside shareholders.

In 1986, after being told that he would not be joining the board until he was forty, he sensed that he needed a greater challenge, so he left to join a merchant bank in London. Two years later, Barlow-Clowes became involved in the buy-out of Buckley. In six short months, the company went from being one of Wales' most profitable companies to being almost bust, and it was put up for sale. Backed by an American venture capital firm, Simon and a group of colleagues valued the business at 97 pence a share. But the wealth of Guinness won the day with a breath-taking offer of £1.47 a share. Club Union Breweries, backed by Harp Lager, which was allied to Guinness bought the company (it became Crown Buckley, and some seven years later, in 1997, it was sold on to Brains).

In 1989, Simon and a group of businessmen bought up Ushers in the West Country for £68 million, the largest brewery buy-out in the history of the brewing industry at the time. The deal involved taking over 433 Courage pubs and a half-million barrel brewery in Trowbridge, a deal that took two years to finalise. Simon hated working for venture capitalists, however, and he gave up after seven months. After a few months' sabbatical he realised that he could never retrieve the family business and decided instead to build himself a small brewery in Llandeilo.

This tied in perfectly with the then Tory Government's Beer Orders, which freed some 20,000 pubs to sell guest beers, thus undoing the ties that the national brewers had enjoyed. This opened the door for small breweries to craft great beers. Simon recalled:

> What triggered it off was when I walked into a pub in Llandeilo – The White Horse – one evening and on the four pumps there wasn't a Welsh cask beer. I said to the licensee at the time, 'Why isn't there a Welsh cask beer?' His answer was, 'There are no Welsh premium beers other than Brains SA.'

This sparked the idea that would become Tomos Watkin, the brewery that Simon would name after a friend who was descended from a Llandovery brewing family. The Castle Hotel in Llandeilo was on the market and Simon bought it and converted garages behind it into a small brewery. The hosting of the National Eisteddfod in the town in 1996 was most fortuitous. This was the brewery's first summer and it launched its first seasonal beer, Cwrw Cayo, for the Eisteddfod. During that festival week some 44,000 pints of Cwrw Cayo were supped.

Simon is modest about the name. He explained to me the origin of the idea:

> I can't take credit for the concept of the name Cwrw Cayo. It was actually a good friend of mine, the late Geoffrey Roy Thomas, a solicitor who had defended members of the Free Wales Army back in 1969 who opened my eyes. Over lunch one day I asked him what I should call the special Eisteddfod beer. He immediately accused me of being silly and of having the obvious name under my very nose. 'Call it Cwrw Cayo,' he said. And since Cayo and I had shared the same godmother, the name was perfect. The rest, as they say, is history.

Simon is ready to admit that it was the success of Cwrw Cayo that made his name as a brewer and also clearly showed him that if you have

Simon Buckley at his Llandeilo brewery

enough cheek to stand up and challenge Welsh people to eat and drink Welsh products, then you will succeed.

From 1996 to 1999 the business was built up, and a new brewery was planned in Llandeilo, but lack of space prevented this. Swansea was chosen instead, which went against Simon's gut feeling. By now, his company Tomos Watkin owned a chain of pubs, most notably The Cayo Arms in Cathedral Road in Cardiff. It became a legend almost overnight. Sadly, as Simon admits, the company did not have enough experience of management to exploit the situation. A group of private investors was brought in and the company's way of working changed from being a cosy family business to being a serious player with outside shareholders.

Then came Foot and Mouth disease, which closed off vast areas of the brewery's catchment area. This meant that between eighty and eighty-five percent of its market was lost. Sales of beer were drastically hit, but as the external directors were based in the south east of England, Foot and Mouth meant nothing to them. Increasingly, Simon was blamed for every failure, and by September 2001 he had simply had enough. He was told by his doctor to take time off work, and during this time, one or two directors tried to take advantage of the situation by getting rid of him, blaming him for the company's situation. He successfully sued them in the High Court. The Tomos Watkin company went into liquidation and then split in two, one with the pubs and the other with the brewery. Shareholders like Simon lost everything – in his case around £1.5 million. He was awarded some £55,000 costs, but by now the company had no money, so he came away saddened, and convinced that if he ever started such a business again, it would never be with external shareholders.

Simon believes that the strong Welsh branding of Tomos Watkin had been directly responsible for Brains' decision to go Welsh in 1995. From being what he describes as 'the cheeky new kid on the block', Tomos Watkin had begun to be seen as a company that stood up and challenged the old values. Simon agrees that Tomos Watkin – and now Evans Evans, the new brewery which he set up in 2004 – are masters of the publicity game. But what might have appeared initially frivolous turned out to be a serious campaign to urge Welsh people to eat Welsh, drink Welsh and be Welsh.

In February 1999, before his departure from the company, another move by Tomos Watkin had been seen as a gimmick, but, according to Simon, it was far from being that. The company launched an audacious hostile bid to buy Brains. Simon and his colleagues managed to raise in excess of £80 million to buy the company, and he believes that five or ten million higher would have clinched the deal:

Examples of Simon Buckley's sense of marketing

What we were going to do was to streamline it, to revitalise it as a company and to turn it into the dynamic drink brand of Wales. To an extent, six or seven years later, they did just that. But I believe we helped. We also planned an ultra-modern brewery just outside Caerffili. Rather than being a huge publicity stunt, we were funded by two big Canadian banks and we were ready to go. And outside our group, there were two Welshmen ready to come in and up the bidding. What Christopher Brain never realised was who was talking to us from his family. To this day, I have never revealed who it was. But the truth of the matter is that we were within six or seven potential points of gaining control. Do I regret not getting my way? It would, no doubt, have made me an extremely wealthy man. But here I am, at 48 years old, absolutely amazed that I am a small company man, my own master and in control of my own destiny. What I have here at Evans Evans is mine. I have more pubs now than I ever had at Tomos Watkin.

After Tomos Watkin, Simon set up the Evan Evans Brewery. He started by buying a pub, The Llannerch Inn at Llandrindod Wells, in 2002. Eighteen months later, along with a business partner, he sold at a significant profit and they were able to set up a new brewery. Thus the Evan Evans Brewery was born. The brewery was named after a family member who once brewed stout in Llanelli.

Evan Evans has the capacity to brew up to six thousand barrels a year. At the top end of the micro, the company is best described as a small regional brewery. This year, the brewing will be up to four thousand barrels. A visitors' centre is planned on the site and the company also plans to launch of a range of seasonal bottled beers and a range of proper Welsh lager, of the type not brewed in Wales since the 1920s. As he explains:

> I want to be remembered when I retire as the man who put the Ale back into Wales, a man who ran good pubs and put the pride back in the brewing industry. And I would like to see my three children continue the Buckley legacy and bring back the crown that rightly belongs to us, that of being the rightful West Wales brewers. What we're about is brewing great beers and offering customers value for money. And encouraging young people to work in the industry. The Buckley brand may now belong to Brains, but the name has never gone away. We are still synonymous with the best brewers in Wales.

Evan Evans' core brands are Cwrw, BB and Warrior. Seasonal ales include Sais Slayer, Dewi Sant, Easter Ale, Cwrw Haf ('Summer Ale' in England), Harvest Home, Full Cry, Bishop's Revenge and Cwrw Santa. Wetherspoons and some of the big pub companies now sell Evan Evans beers. Around thirty per cent of production sells outside Wales.

Simon admits that he has survived some dark days, but one day, when things were looking grim, he was heartened by a comment made by the Vicar of Llangadog, Michael Cottam:

> 'Remember this, Simon,' he said. 'The good Lord put eyes in the front of your head for a very good reason – look forward. You are well known in the market place. Go out and do it.'

Today, Evan Evans has a state of the art brewery with a choice of beers ranging from a 3.8 Best Bitter to the CAMRA gold medal award-winning 4.2 Cwrw. The brewery employs nine people and owns or is negotiating to buy eleven pubs. At the time of going to press, Evan Evans was about to open a pub named Y Cadno (The Fox) a few doors away from the famous Cayo Arms. Simon expects it to repeat the success that The Cayo enjoyed. The sign will read 'Cofiwch Cayo – The Fox Returns'.

Chapter 14

No Small Beer

Commercial brewing in Wales gradually dwindled until fairly recently, when dozens of small, micro and cottage breweries emerged. Unfortunately, the larger breweries had become so powerful that many of these smaller enterprises were short-lived and most of them had gone to the wall by the 1990s. Today it is estimated that some five hundred exist throughout the United Kingdom. Their output is small, on average around 500 to 600 gallons a week and on a UK scale this represents only two percent of the beer market. They do provide a wider choice than ever before, however.

The Guinness Book of Records claims that the world's smallest brewery is to be found at Ty'n Llidiart in Capel Bangor near Aberystwyth. It has managed to remain despite the fact that the adjacent pub was forced to close because of high overheads and too low a turnover. Then it was taken over by a local couple, Mark and Margaret Phillips. The loft was turned into a restaurant and in June 2002 the pub opened its own brewery named the Gwynant Brewery. It proudly boasts a certificate from Guinness confirming its status as the smallest in the world. It measures ten feet

Ty'n Llidiart, Capel Bangor near Aberystwyth, the smallest brewery in the world

Two rustics enjoying Small Beer. Note the Brecknockshire caps.

high, is only five feet square, and serves as a popular tourist attraction.

This tiny brewery is not, however, a mere gimmick. The building was once the pub's toilet and now brews high quality beer. The pub also stocks guest beers from all over Wales and beyond. It is ironic that in the building where male customers once got rid of what beer produces, beer is now produced. Indeed, the original name of the brewery was Bragdy Tŷ Bach, or the 'Toilet Brewery'. Brewer Chris Giles, who also runs a real ale distribution company involving some twenty-five small and micro breweries, has the experience and background that allows him to experiment with different varieties of hops. His main brew is Cwrw Gwynant, and he brews nine gallons once a week. He designed the brewing equipment, and his product is free from sugar and of any added chemicals. The brewing takes around five and a half hours. Then the beer ferments for three or four days, and is kept in its barrel for around a fortnight before being sold.

Bragdy Gwynant is living proof that bigger doesn't necessarily mean better. Ty'n Llidiart won the CAMRA award as Ceredigion's Best Pub for its provision of real ale, which includes Cwrw Gwynant.

Bragdy Gwynant is not the only small brewery in Ceredigion, however. At Pentregât near New Quay a small company has adopted the county name. The Ceredigion Brewery is a five-barrel affair set up in an old barn at Wervil Grange. Hops of the highest quality are used to brew Y Barcud Coch, Black Witch, Blodeuwedd, Y Ddraig Aur and Old Black Bull, which is a strong stout with an alcohol content of 6.2 percent.

Nearby at Llanarth, the Pen-lôn Cottage Brewery produces bottled all-grain beers listed as Ewes Frolic Lager, Lamb's Gold Light Ale, Ramnesia Strong Ale, Stock Ram Stout, Tipsy Tup Pale Ale, and Twin Ram India Pale Ale, which earned a True Taste Commendation for 2005/6. Stefan and Penny Samociuk grow their own hops and use old Welsh species of barley, including Hen Haidd Enlli (Old Bardsey Barley).

Up north, in Porthmadog, the Pink Moose Brewery opened in June 2005. This ten-barrel venture is to be commended for its wise drinking campaign, which encourages drinkers not to over-indulge. It produces three regular beers: Cwrw Madog and Cwrw Glaslyn, both bitter, and Ochr Dywyll y Mŵs (The Dark Side of the Moose), a dark beer. These are also available in bottles. Seasonal beers include X-Mŵs Llawen for Christmas, Cwrw Dewi Da for St David's Day, and Cwrw'r Pasg for Easter.

Still further north, Bragdy Ynys Môn was founded in 1999 at Talwrn, the first to be established in the area since 1984. The company produces brews named Amnesia, Enlli, Medra, Môn Seiriol, Seuruik, Sirol, Chwerw

Sospan Fach, Stowt Tarw Du (Black Bull Stout) and Wennol (Swallow). Further along the north Wales coast, the Conway Brewery is located in the Morfa area of Conwy. It provides both barrel and bottled beers and mainly supplies north east Wales. Conway Brewery beers are stocked at the Castle in Conwy and at Cobdens in Capel Curig. Its beers include Castle Bitter, Cwrw Mêl (Honey Beer) and Arbennig (Special), which is a dark. It also provides seasonal beers such as Haul Dawns (Sun Dance), with an alcohol content of 4 percent.

The Gogarth, or the Great Orme Brewery was set up in an old cowshed at Glan Conwy. Its 'Extravaganza' won the prize for the Champion Beer at the Leeds Beer, Cider and Perry Festival in 2006.

Denbigh, a town with a fine tradition of brewing, has its own brewery after some fifteen lean years. Bragdy'r Bryn was opened by Geraint Roberts in the summer of 2005 on the Colomendy Estate. He started with a ten-barrel weekly production but it seems that this will have to be doubled.

Plassey Beer is brewed at Plassey near Wrexham, and here you may still buy lager bearing the Wrexham name – the Royal Wrexham Lager. The company was founded in 1985 by the late Alan Beresford, who was previously a brewer at the Border Brewery in Wrexham. The brewery has a viewing gallery as well as a company shop. Plassey can also boast the triple crown, as it won the Welsh Beer Championship three times in a row between 1995 and 1997. The brewery produces the award-winning Dragon's Breath (Anadl y Ddraig), a bitter, and developed the Fusilier, available in barrel and bottle, as the regimental ale for the Welsh Fusiliers. It also brews Cwrw Tudno, with a strength of five per cent.

Although Wrexham itself has seen all its large breweries disappear, Pene (Penelope) Coles runs her own small plant, the Jolly Brewer, in the town. Supplying her own catering business in the main, Jolly Brewer produces beers with such eccentric names as Taffy's Tipple, Dusky Maiden, Jolly Dark Lager, Lucinda's Lager, Taid's Fragrant Garden, Strange Brew and Diod y Grynaes (which seems like a corruption of Gymraes). As previously noted, Pene is also connected with a brewing venture launched by supporters of Wrexham Football Club.

Back in mid Wales, the Breconshire Brewery was opened in 2002 on the Ffrwgrech Estate at Brecon by C.H. Marlow, a well-established distribution company. This ten-barrel business uses equipment from the old Pembrokeshire Brewery. The head brewer, Justin 'Buster' Grant, has an MSc degree in brewing and distilling, and thanks to the efforts of local MP and Assembly Member David Davies, the brewery's product is now available at the Welsh Assembly's bar.

Bottled beer from some of the home and micro breweries, for sale at Blas ar Win, Llanrwst

The brewery has regularly won prizes for its products, taking the award for Wales' best bitter twice in successive years. It brews Brecon County Ale, Golden Valley, Red Dragon, Ramblers Ruin, Brecknock Best, Fan Dance, which is a seasonal beer, and The Spirit of the Dragon.

Down further to the south-east, the Cwmbran Brewery below Maen Mountain was founded in 1994, and the business was licensed two years later. Initially, Martin Lewis and Keith Gullick began with only one kind of beer, looking to develop gradually. They brewed for the community, following a centuries-old tradition of brewing locally. The business has developed, and the company now produces some fifteen different brews, and its product has broken through to chains such as Wetherspoons, Sainsbury and Tesco.

The company's main brew is Crow Valley, which is available in barrel and in bottle. It also brews Deryn Du (Blackbird) stout, which has a taste of blackberry. The product varies from between 3.5 to 5 percent ABV.

The Rhymney Brewery was revived in 2005. This was made possible by an investment package of £313,000 made through Finance Wales and a Welsh Assembly grant, together with a personal investment by the founders, father and son Steve and Marc Evans.

Located at the heads of the valleys on the Pant Estate at Dowlais, the

The Tomos Watkin Brewery presented a milestone in the history of the smaller breweries.

company concentrates on hand-crafted beer and already it has succeeded in breaking through into supplying chain outlets such as Wetherspoons, Asda and Spar. Recently the company exported five thousand bottles to the Ukraine.

The company's brews include Bevan's Bitter, named after the founder of the National Health Service, and Centenary 1905, which marked the hundredth anniversary of the granting of a Royal Charter to Merthyr, when Keir Hardie presented Cyfarthfa Castle to the townspeople. Rhymney Brewery also produces a lager.

One of the company's most popular lines is the mini-can, designed as a small keg and containing five litres of beer. The Rhymney Brewery recently announced plans for installing a fully automatic bottling plant.

The Carreg Brewing Company was set up at Treorchi in the Rhondda in 2004 with the intent of producing Pilsner lager. During its first year, the company's product was sold from the Guinness and Brains beer buses on the National Eisteddfod field at Newport. The company's bottled beer sells at such eateries as Le Gallois, Blas and Capital Cuisine in Cardiff.

The Warcop Brewery was set up in an old milking parlour in 1999 on the coast of Gwent at Wentloog, between Cardiff and Newport. The name of the business is an acronym taken from family members' initials: (W)illiam, husband, (Ann), wife, (R)hian, daughter, (C)eri, daughter, (O)wain, son, and (P)icton, the family surname. Originally, the family had considered opening a brewery in Moscow, but a start was made in Gwent in order to gain experience in the business and to test the water, as it were. The founder, William Picton, has a degree in chemistry and he has specialised in genetic enzymes, and spent five years working in Moscow. Warcop's products are distributed mainly in the Gwent and Cardiff areas, with over two dozen brews divided into five categories based on different kinds of hops: dark bitter, dark mild, lager and various strong beers for special occasions. The beers vary in strength from Pit Shaft, with 3.4 percent, to Deep Pit, at 5 percent.

One of Wales' most successful small breweries is the Bulmastiff Brewery in Cardiff. It should be recognisable to viewers of S4C as the brewery used for the Cic Mul (Mule's Kick Brewery) used in the Welsh-language soap opera Pobol y Cwm. The brewery was originally founded at Penarth by milkman Bob Jenkins in 1987. He bought the brewing plant from Monmouth Fine Ales and named his business after his dogs. It was a natural step, therefore, to name one of his beers Son of a Bitch. This brew won a Silver Medal at the London Beer Festival in 1996. The company also won the national first prize both in 1999 and in 2000 for its Golden Brew. It was still winning medals in 2005. Among its other brews are Best Bitter, Snarlsberg Lager, Thoroughbred and Brindle. Seasonal brews include Summer Moult and Mogadog. In 1992 Bob moved his business to a larger site at Grangetown together with his brother Paul, expanding to a twenty-barrel production per week and supplying some thirty pubs.

The Bryncelyn Brewery, located in the Swansea Valley, is no ordinary affair. Bryncelyn, which means Holly Hill, is dedicated to the memory of Buddy Holly. It was set up as a one-barrel brewery at the Wern Fawr pub in Ystalyfera by Will Hopton, a Buddy Holly fanatic, together with his wife Sandra and a local regular, Robert Scott.

The brewery kicked off with Buddy's Delight but it subsequently expanded its production to a dozen different brews, three of which are regular brews, while the remaining ones are specials. Bryncelyn has captured a number of CAMRA awards and the Wern Fawr was named Pub of the Year by the local branch of CAMRA, as well as being named

CAMRA's Best Regional Pub for 2005.

The brewery's offerings include Buddy Marvellous, Oh Boy, Holly Hop, Peggy's Brew, Buddy's Delight, Cwrw Celyn, CHH, Rave On, Buddy Confusing, Feb '59, May B Baby and That'll Be the Sleigh.

Another Swansea-area company is the Swansea Brewing Company, whose base is a pub, The Joiners Arms, in Bishopston. Four varieties of beer are produced: Deep Slade Dark, Bishopswood Bitter, Three Cliffs Gold and Original Wood, the latter with an alcohol content of 5.2 percent. Swansea Brewing Company began as a two-barrel brewery in April 1996 but managed to double production by the end of its first year.

In 1996, the Tomos Watkin Brewery, discussed in the previous chapter, was founded behind the Castle pub in Llandeilo. After the squabble between Simon Buckley and the board in 2002, Tomos Watkin was taken over by the Hurns company. A new brewery was built at Swansea as part of a £10 million expansion plan. It continues brewing Cwrw Haf (Summer Beer); Stowt Myrddin (Merlin's Stout), which won the Welsh CAMRA Award in 2005; OSB Bitter; Whoosh, which is a dark yellow beer, and Watkin BB, a traditional bitter.

Two pubs sharing the same name also double as breweries. One is the White Hart at Machen near Caerffili and the other is the White Hart at Llanddarog. At Llanddarog, Cwrw Blasus is brewed on premises that date back to 1371. The Carter Brewery at Machen dates back to 1794 and has an interesting wooden panel saved from the liner The Empress of France, which was scrapped in 1960.

Back up north, at Waunfawr, at the Snowdonia Park, traditional beer including Welsh Highland Bitter is brewed to commemorate the re-opening of the Highland Railway in August 2000. One of the narrow gauge line's little stations stands nearby.

Despite the fact that only two large breweries remain in Wales, the choice on offer is wider than ever. The smaller breweries are now the front runners in the trade as far as choice and taste is concerned. Good beer, cider and whisky are all within reach. But there is still room for improvement. I can but agree with this comment in CAMRA's *2006 Real Ale Pub Guide:*

A pub that doesn't sell real ale is not easy to excuse, but is at least easy to avoid. A pub that sells real ale badly seems to me to be committing a much greater crime.

Amen, say I.